Rhymes
for the Times
Literacy Strategies through Social Studies

Authors

Timothy Rasinski, Ph.D.

David L. Harrison, Litt.D.

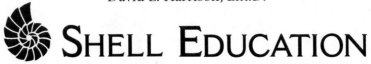

SHELL EDUCATION

Publishing Credits

Corinne Burton, M.A.Ed., *President*; Wendy Conklin, M.A., *Contributing Author*; Kristin Kemp, M.A.Ed., *Contributing Author*; Emily R. Smith, M.A.Ed., *Content Director*; Jennifer Wilson, *Senior Editor*; Robin Erickson, *Multimedia Designer*; Don Tran, *Production Artist*; Stephanie Bernard, *Assistant Editor*; Valerie Morales, *Assistant Editor*

Image Credits

Page 155, Alamy; all other images Shutterstock and iStock.

Standards

© 2007 Teachers of English to Speakers of Other Languages, Inc. (TESOL)
© 2007 Board of Regents of the University of Wisconsin System. World-Class Instructional Design and Assessment (WIDA)
© Copyright 2010. National Governors Association Center for Best Practices and Council of Chief State School Officers. All rights reserved.

Shell Education
5301 Oceanus Drive
Huntington Beach, CA 92649-1030
http://www.shelleducation.com
ISBN 978-1-4258-1467-0
© 2016 Shell Educational Publishing, Inc.

Table of Contents

A Perfect Match—
Poetry and Reading

I'm a reading guy. Specifically, I am interested in how children learn to read and what we as teachers and parents can do to nurture students' reading development and their love of reading. I am particularly interested in helping those students who find learning to read difficult and who as a result tend to dislike reading. For these students, as well as the normal, achieving, and advanced readers, poetry is an ideal text. Let me explain why.

Poems are generally not lengthy. Students can read (and master) them rather quickly. The length of a book, or even a chapter, may intimidate some students. Poems are welcoming texts. It is not difficult for students, even those who struggle the most in reading, to achieve success in reading poetry.

Poems are fun to read. The rhythm, rhyme, and wordplay embedded in most poems allow students to involve their whole bodies and voices in the reading. It is rewarding to watch students sway their bodies, stomp their feet, clap their hands, and bob their heads as they read poetry. Clearly, they find ways to enjoy reading poems.

Words are important when it comes to reading. Poets are very careful in the words they choose. The words found in poems are sure to increase students' vocabularies and give students opportunities to explore rhyme, alliteration, metaphor, simile, and many other forms of figurative language.

Poems are meant to be performed orally and therefore need to be rehearsed. Rehearsal, or the repeated reading of a text, is a powerful way to build word recognition, improve reading fluency, and enhance reading comprehension—three of the most important components in the reading process.

Learning is always better when it is done with others. (I love working with my good friend, renowned poet David Harrison.) It is meant to be a collaborative experience. Poetry can be performed by one, two, three, or more students. And, there should always be an audience to listen to the performers.

Finally, the content of a poem can set the stage for further learning. Reading, rereading, and performing the wonderful poems in this book will build interest and background in a variety of social studies topics that will lead students to even deeper exploration and learning on the topics.

We have used poetry in the Kent State University reading clinic for years. Every day, students learn to read and perform new poems (or songs). Not only have we seen remarkable growth in students' proficiency in reading, but we also see great improvements in their love of reading and in their own confidence as readers. Poetry for the sake of poetry is wonderful in itself. Poetry as a vehicle for growing readers is an added bonus.

David and I believe you and your students will love the poetry in this book, learn more about America and the world than you knew before, and help your students become better and more motivated readers.

Wishing you all the best,

Timothy Rasinski, Ph.D.
Professor of Reading Education
Member, International Reading Hall of Fame
Kent State University

Why Poetry?

A Poet's Perspective

I spend most days writing. My favorite form is poetry. Poetry fits me like my skin. Its forehead wrinkles when I frown. It chortles when I'm tickled, sniffles when I'm sad. Poetry is not my second self, it is myself—changeable, curious, timid, bold, passionate, fearful, triumphant. And did I mention silly? No other genre can be as lighthearted, funny, or downright silly as a poem.

No wonder, then, that kids who are properly introduced to poetry greet it like the good friend and guide it is. Poetry can, should, and often does speak a universal language that young people understand. Children like to laugh. So does poetry. Children connect to poems that relate to them—their lives, experiences, hopes, and dreams. Poetry takes them on unexpected adventures, shows them sights they've never seen, and holds up the prism of life itself so that they can see all its colors and possibilities.

So, why poetry? Why here in this book on social studies? Because poems can also stimulate a desire to know more and set the stage for classroom study and discussion. If a poem tells you that Rhode Island is small but thinks big, you want to know exactly why and how it thinks big. A poem that tells you we came close to calling our presidents "Excellency" or "His Highness" makes you want to ask about the origins of other traditions. A 107-word history lesson can make us think about what life was like in Egypt 10,000 years before the pharaohs and pyramids came on the scene.

Tim Rasinski has spent his professional career examining the ways in which young people master language and become successful learners. Again and again, the use of poetry to support learning emerges as one of the most effective classroom strategies we have. Poetry is honest and gets straight to the heart of the matter. It can be as personal as a text or as public as a post on the Internet. It's from me to you, telling you that I've studied the situation, thought about it, and this is what I found out.

Why poetry? Why not?

David L. Harrison, Litt.D.
Poet Laureate
Drury University

Why Poetry? *(cont.)*

A Student's Perspective

Why poetry?

A poem is not just
Words on a page.
A poem is a gift
A poet gives to my soul.

Poetry is not
A prize to be won,
But a secret
To be unlocked.

Poetry is beautiful,
Horrible,
Light,
And dark.

Poetry is a breathtaking,
Tornado of emotions.

Why poetry?

Poetry is music.
Each word has its own rhythm,
Each stanza
Is a new verse.

When children
Listen to poetry,
It's like a mental movie
That is set to music.

Poems help imaginations wander
And creativity soar.

Why poetry?

So why poetry?
That is the question.
And why, of all things,
In social studies?

History is not facts.
History is stories.
History has a plot, climax, characters,
And drama.

Poetry is music.
History is a movie.
Together, they make
A musical—

A musical where children
Absorb information like sponges.

Why poetry?

Poetry tells a story
Unlike anything else,
A vivid description,
Not a bland tale.

No child likes
Listening to boring facts.
But listening to exciting stories?
That gets kids pumped up.

Help children find their voices.
Poetry opens a world of possibilities.

Kiley E. Smith
Middle School Student in Virginia

Why This Book?

This book was developed in response to the need from teachers for good texts for teaching reading fluency within the content areas, such as social studies. Fluency has become recognized as an essential element in elementary and middle-grade reading programs. The review of research by the National Reading Panel (2000) and others (e.g., Rasinski and Hoffman 2003) confirms that fluency is absolutely essential to reading success. Fluent readers are better able to comprehend what they read. They decode words so effortlessly that they can devote their cognitive resources to comprehension instead of bogging themselves down in decoding words they confront in their reading. They can also construct meaning (comprehension) by reading with appropriate expression and phrasing (Hackett 2013).

Readers develop fluency through guided practice and repeated readings with appropriate expression and phrasing. Regular repeated readings under the guidance and assistance of a teacher or other coach improves word recognition, reading rate, comprehension, and overall reading proficiency.

Rereading, Close Reading, and Practice

Students will find the poems in this book interesting and sometimes challenging. They will especially want to practice the poems if you provide regular opportunities to perform for their classmates, parents, or other audiences. So, have fun with these poems. Be assured that if you regularly have your students read and perform the poems in this book, you will go a long way toward developing fluent readers who are able to decode words effortlessly and construct meaning through their interpretations of texts. And as our student poet so clearly shared on page 7, students will enjoy hearing the stories of history through poetry.

Poems should be interpreted with meaning as the foremost guiding principle. Students should read to the punctuation as opposed to line-by-line. If you choose to divide the selections into parts, they should be divided with close attention to meaningful phrases and thoughts rather than just by the layout of the text.

The poems should be read repeatedly, or closely, over several days for expression and meaning. We recommend that you introduce one poem at a time and practice it over the next three, four, or five days, depending on how quickly your students develop mastery of it. Write the poem you are going to read on chart paper or project a digital copy of the poem. (Digital copies of the poems are provided online. See page 12 for more information.)

Why This Book? *(cont.)*

Rereading, Close Reading, and Practice *(cont.)*

Have students read the poem several times each day. They should read it a couple times at the beginning of each day, read it several times during various breaks in the day, and read it multiple times at the end of each day. For middle school students, encourage students to practice the poem at home since they do not have much time in your class during the day.

Make two copies of the poem for each student. Have students keep one copy at school in their "fluency and poetry folders." The other copy can be sent home for the students to practice with their families. Communicate to families the importance of children continuing to practice the poems at home with their family members.

Coaching Your Students

A key ingredient to repeated reading is the coaching that comes from a teacher. Students who hear and talk about fluent reading from and with more proficient readers develop a better understanding of fluent reading (Oczkus and Rasinski 2015). As your students practice reading the target poem each week alone, in small groups, or as an entire class, be sure to provide positive feedback about their reading. Help them develop a sense for reading the poem in such a way that it shares the meaning that the author attempts to convey or the meaning that the reader may wish to convey. Through oral interpretation of a poem, readers can express joy, sadness, anger, surprise, or any of a variety of emotions. Help students learn to use their reading to express this level of meaning.

Teachers do this by listening from time to time as students read and coaching them in the various aspects of oral interpretation. You may wish to suggest that students emphasize certain words, insert dramatic pauses, read a bit faster in one place, or slow down in other parts of the poem. And of course, lavish praise on students' best efforts to convey a sense of meaning through their reading. Although it may take a while for the students to learn to develop this sense of voice in their reading, in the long run, it will lead to more engaged and fluent reading and higher levels of comprehension.

How to Use This Resource

This book is divided into two main sections. The first half of the book includes the strategy model lessons and example lessons. The second half of the book includes 60 phenomenal social studies-based poems written by David L. Harrison.

Strategy Lessons

Model Lesson—Each strategy starts with a teacher lesson plan. The strategy is described with guidance for what teachers should do to prepare students for the strategy. The lesson is written to be used with any poem or other verse text of your choice.

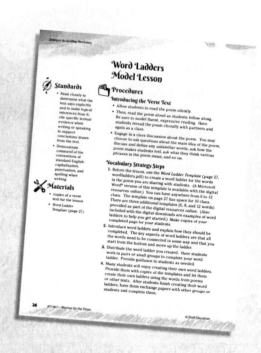

Template—For each strategy, a template of the necessary student page is provided for your use. The templates are available as Adobe® PDFs with the digital resources online. If you would like to customize the templates to different verse texts, these pages are also provided as Microsoft Word® files and (See page 12 for more information.)

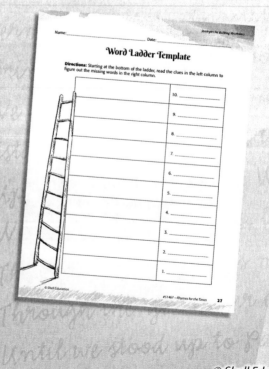

How to Use This Resource (cont.)

Example Lesson—For each strategy, there is also an example lesson featuring one of David L. Harrison's poems from the poetry collection in this book. This allows you to see the concrete application of the abstract model lesson. You can then take this lesson and use it with one of the other poems in this collection or with poems from other poets.

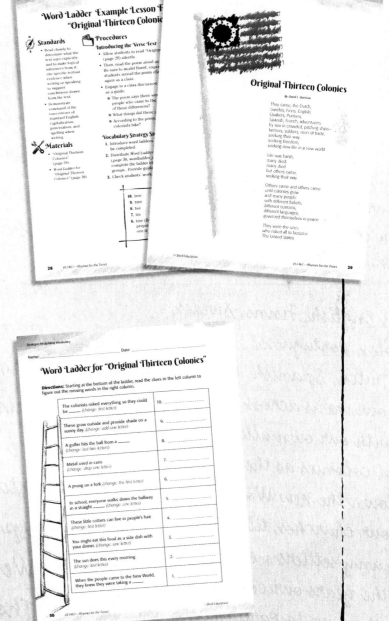

Student Pages—Any needed student pages are provided for the example lesson. These are good examples for what the templates should look like after you prepare them for your students. These pages are provided as Adobe® PDFs with the Digital Resources Online. (See page 12 for more information.)

How to Use This Resource (cont.)

Poetry Collection

Poems About the 50 United States—This section includes background information and 20 poems about the 50 states. Students will enjoy learning about various regions of the United States as they read these clever poems.

Poems About American History—Within this section are 20 poems and background information about American history through the 1800s. Students will learn about history through the voices of people.

Poems About Ancient Civilizations—There are 20 poems and background information about the various ancient civilizations in this section. Whether it is the ancient Chinese or the ancient Greeks, students will be fascinated by Harrison's poetic descriptions.

Digital Resources Online

The templates and poems in this book are available as Microsoft Word® files and/or Adobe® PDFs online. A complete list of the available documents is available on pages 167–168. Additionally, each lesson page includes the file names of the documents needed for the lesson. To access the digital resources, go to www.tcmpub.com/download-files and enter the following code: 70060511. Then, follow the on-screen directions.

References Cited

Hackett, Kelly. 2013. *Ready! Set! Go! Literacy Centers*. Huntington Beach, CA: Shell Education.

Ozckus, Lori, and Timothy Rasinski. 2015. *Close Reading with Paired Texts*. Huntington Beach, CA: Shell Education.

Rasinski, Timothy, and James Hoffman. 2003. "Theory and Research into Practice: Oral Reading in the School Literacy Curriculum." *Reading Research Quarterly* 38: 510–522.

Strategies for Building Fluency

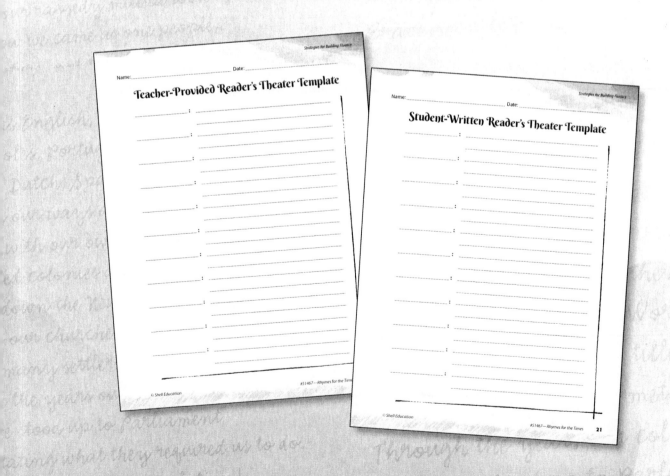

Teacher-Provided Reader's Theater Model Lesson

Standards

- Determine central ideas or themes of a text and analyze their development; summarize the key supporting details and ideas.
- Read closely to determine what the text says explicitly and to make logical inferences from it; cite specific textual evidence when writing or speaking to support conclusions drawn from the text.

Materials

- copies of a verse text for the lesson
- *Teacher-Provided Reader's Theater Template* (page 15)

Procedures

Introducing the Verse Text

- Allow students to read the poem silently.
- Then, read the poem aloud as students follow along. Be sure to model fluent, expressive reading. Have students reread the poem chorally with partners and again as a class.
- Engage in a class discussion about the poem. You may choose to ask questions about the main idea of the poem, discuss and define any unfamiliar words, ask how the poem makes students feel, ask what they think various phrases in the poem mean, and so on.

Fluency Strategy Steps

1. Before the lesson, create a script about the verse text using the *Teacher-Provided Reader's Theater Template* (page 15, teacherstheater.pdf). (A Microsoft Word® version of this template is available with the digital resources online.) Then, distribute copies of the script. There may not be enough parts for every student in your class, so you may need to divide your students into groups. Be sure to think about the number of parts before assigning them to students.

2. Have students rehearse the script several times in small groups to enhance listening and speaking skills and to improve fluency and confidence.

3. Do not require students to memorize the text for the performance, but instead ask that they be prepared to read it aloud with confidence and with good expression.

4. Students may perform a reading for classmates, parents, the school principal, other teachers or classes. Alternatively, they could record their performance and share it online.

Name:_____ Date: _____

Teacher-Provided Reader's Theater Template

_____ : _____
                   _____

_____ : _____
                   _____

_____ : _____
                   _____

_____ : _____
                   _____

_____ : _____
                   _____

_____ : _____
                   _____

_____ : _____
                   _____

_____ : _____
                   _____

_____ : _____
                   _____

_____ : _____
                   _____

Teacher-Provided Reader's Theater
Example Lesson Featuring "Arkansas"

Standards

- Determine central ideas or themes of a text and analyze their development; summarize the key supporting details and ideas.

- Read closely to determine what the text says explicitly and to make logical inferences from it; cite specific textual evidence when writing or speaking to support conclusions drawn from the text.

Materials

- "Arkansas" (page 17)
- *Reader's Theater for "Arkansas"* (page 18)

Procedures

Introducing the Verse Text

- Allow students to read "Arkansas" (page 17) silently.
- Then, read the poem aloud as students follow along. Be sure to model fluent, expressive reading.
- Have students reread the poem chorally with partners and again as a class.
- Engage in a class discussion using the following questions as a guide:
  - ✱ Based on the poem, what kinds of things would you expect to see in Arkansas?
  - ✱ How did Arkansas get its name?
  - ✱ What does the phrase "My history runs deep" mean in the poem?

Fluency Strategy Steps

1. Distribute *Reader's Theater for "Arkansas"* (page 18, readerstheater_arkansas.pdf). There are four parts in this reader's theater script. Divide your students into groups of four to perform this reader's theater.

2. Have students rehearse the script several times in small groups to enhance listening and speaking skills and to improve fluency and confidence.

3. Do not require students to memorize the text for the performance, but instead ask that they be prepared to read it aloud with confidence and with good expression.

4. Have groups of students perform the reader's theater script for other classes in the school that are studying the states.

Arkansas

By David L. Harrison

Akakaze—
To the Quapaw it meant
"land of downriver people."
To the Dakota, it was
"people of the south wind."
The French pronounced it
Arcansas,
and so I was named.

My history runs deep
as limestone frosted caves
beneath my valleys,
clear as waterfalls plunging
into cold streams,
wild as bear, bobcat, elk,
nimble as a white-tailed deer.

I was proud to be America's
twenty-fifth state.
Come float my streams,
enjoy my beauty
in Arkansas.

Name:_____ Date: _____

Reader's Theater for "Arkansas"

All: *Akakaze*

Reader 1: You might wonder, what does it mean?

All: To the Quapaw it meant "land of downriver people."

Reader 2: The Quapaw tribe lived in Arkansas.

Reader 3: They traveled down the Mississippi River from Ohio to get there.

Reader 4: That's why they named it

All: "land of the downriver people."

Reader 1: The Dakota Indians lived just north of Arkansas.

Reader 2: They had their own meaning for the word, *Akakaze.*

All: To the Dakota, it was "people of the south wind."

Reader 3: This was their name for anyone who lived south of them.

Reader 4: And so, Akakaze was the name they gave to the Quapaw Indians.

All: The French pronounced it *Arcansas*.

Reader 1: The French were the first white people to settle in Arkansas.

Reader 2: They named it after the word for the Quapaw Indians.

All: and so I was named.

Reader 3: Arkansas has a deep history.

Reader 4: Hernando de Soto was the first European explorer to visit.

Reader 1: He was searching for gold and a passageway to the far East.

Reader 2: French people settled the land.

Reader 3: More people came to settle, too.

Reader 4: Then, the United States bought Arkansas in the Louisiana Purchase.

All: My history runs deep as limestone frosted caves beneath my valleys.

Reader 1: Just below the ground in Arkansas

Reader 2: lies a beautiful scene of limestone caves.

Reader 3: Inside these caves you will see streams flowing.

Reader 4: Crystals sparkle and fossils reveal what was there long ago.

Reader 1: Salamanders slither and blind fish swim.

Name:_____ Date:_____

Reader's Theater for "Arkansas" *(cont.)*

Reader 2: Each cave is a living cave.

Reader 3: This means it is changing day by day.

Reader 4: It is a magical underground place.

All: My history runs clear as waterfalls plunging into cold streams.

Reader 1: The waterfalls in Arkansas are amazing to see.

Reader 2: They are found in the mountains that cover much of the state.

Reader 3: Some are tall and cascade down cliffs.

Reader 4: Others are wide, shallow falls that flow into streams.

All: My history runs wild as bear, bobcat, elk.

Reader 1: Long ago, there were so many black bears

Reader 2: that the state was nicknamed "The Bear State."

Reader 3: Long-legged bobcats hunt the land

Reader 4: for a dinner of rodents, rabbits, and small birds.

Reader 1: Elk is the largest animal found in Arkansas.

Reader 2: If you are lucky, you can spot them in a national park or near a river.

All: My history runs nimble as a white-tailed deer.

Reader 3: This is Arkansas's state mammal.

Reader 4: Underneath its tail is white.

Reader 1: It waves as it runs more than 40 miles per hour!

Reader 2: When danger is near, it flashes as a warning sign.

All: I was proud to be America's twenty-fifth state.

Reader 3: This happened in 1836.

Reader 4: It had been just a territory before that.

Readers 1 & 2: Come float my streams,

Readers 3 & 4: enjoy my beauty

All: in Arkansas.

Student-Written Reader's Theater Model Lesson

Standards

- Determine central ideas or themes of a text and analyze their development; summarize the key supporting details and ideas.
- Produce clear and coherent writing in which the development, organization, and style are appropriate to task, purpose, and audience.

Materials

- copies of a verse text for the lesson
- reader's theater example script
- *Student-Written Reader's Theater Template* (page 21)

Procedures

Introducing the Verse Text

- Allow students to read the poem silently.
- Then, read the poem aloud as students follow along. Be sure to model fluent, expressive reading. Have students reread the poem chorally in small groups.
- Engage in a class discussion about the poem. You may choose to ask questions about the main idea of the poem, discuss and define any unfamiliar words, ask how the poem makes students feel, ask what they think various phrases in the poem mean, and so on.

Fluency Strategy Steps

1. Provide students with copies of *Reader's Theater for "Arkansas"* (pages 18–19, readerstheater_arkansas.pdf) or another example reader's theater. (There are a few other examples provided as part of the digital resources online.) These scripts serve as examples to help guide students in writing their own reader's theater scripts. Call students' attention to the number of parts, how many lines there are per reader, and the length of the script. Have students take notes about how they can incorporate some of the same aspects into their own scripts.

2. Distribute the *Student-Written Reader's Theater Template* (page 21, studenttheater.pdf). (A Microsoft Word® version of this template is available with the digital resources online.) Have students write their own reader's theater scripts to go with the verse text you are using for this lesson. Encourage additional research about the poem's topic. Students may even choose to focus on a specific topic from the poem. Have students work independently or in small groups.

3. Have students rehearse the reader's theater script several times in small groups to enhance fluency and to improve students' confidence and expression.

4. Encourage students to perform their reader's theater scripts for classmates, parents, or other teachers or classes. Alternatively, they could record their performance and share it online.

Name:_____ Date: _____

Student-Written Reader's Theater Template

_____ : _____

_____

_____ : _____

_____

_____ : _____

_____

_____ : _____

_____

_____ : _____

_____

_____ : _____

_____

_____ : _____

_____

_____ : _____

_____

_____ : _____

_____

_____ : _____

_____

Student-Written Reader's Theater Example Lesson Featuring "Puritan Woman"

Standards

- Determine central ideas or themes of a text and analyze their development; summarize the key supporting details and ideas.
- Produce clear and coherent writing in which the development, organization, and style are appropriate to task, purpose, and audience.

Materials

- "Puritan Woman" (page 23)
- *Reader's Theater for "Puritan Woman"* (page 24)

Procedures

Introducing the Verse Text

- Allow students to read "Puritan Woman" (page 23) silently.
- Then, read the poem aloud as students follow along. Be sure to model fluent, expressive reading. Have students reread the poem chorally in small groups.
- Engage in a class discussion using the following questions as a guide:
  ＊ What makes a Puritan woman's life hard?
  ＊ How is a Puritan woman similar to and different from a modern woman?
  ＊ What do you think "weighty matters" might mean?

Fluency Strategy Steps

1. Provide students with copies of *Reader's Theater for "Arkansas"* (pages 18–19, readerstheater_arkansas.pdf) or another example reader's theater (readerstheater_examples.pdf). These scripts serve as examples to help guide students in writing their own reader's theater scripts. Call students' attention to the number of parts, how many lines there are per reader, and the length of the script. Have students take notes about how they can incorporate some of the same aspects into their own scripts.

2. Distribute multiple copies of *Reader's Theater for "Puritan Woman"* (page 24, readerstheater_puritan.pdf) to each student. Have students write their own reader's theater scripts to retell "Puritan Woman." Encourage additional research about the poem's topic of women during the colonial times. Students may choose to focus on specific topics in the poem, such as child-rearing, chores, or suffrage. You may choose to have students work independently or in small groups.

3. Have students rehearse their reader's theater scripts several times in small groups to enhance fluency and improve students' confidence and expression.

4. Set up opportunities for the students to perform their reader's theater scripts for the librarian or media specialist.

Puritan Woman

By David L. Harrison

I am a Puritan woman.
My job is to obey my husband,
bear his children, raise them to be
obedient, God-fearing boys and girls.

Is life hard?
Oftentimes it seems so.
Last week I buried my oldest.
Sat some time in silence,
but there was much to do
besides mourning.

My job is to spin yarn from wool,
knit our sweaters and stockings,
make soap, dip candles,
churn cream into butter,
prepare food for the table.

I'm not allowed to own so much
as the clothes upon my back.
I cannot vote on colony affairs.
My husband attends
to such weighty matters.

Is life hard?
Oftentimes it seems so.
I am a Puritan woman.

Name: _____ Date: _____

Reader's Theater for "Puritan Woman"

Directions: Write a reader's theater script about the poem "Puritan Woman."

_____ : _____

_____

_____ : _____

_____

_____ : _____

_____

_____ : _____

_____

_____ : _____

_____

_____ : _____

_____

_____ : _____

_____

_____ : _____

_____

_____ : _____

_____

_____ : _____

_____

Strategies for Building Vocabulary

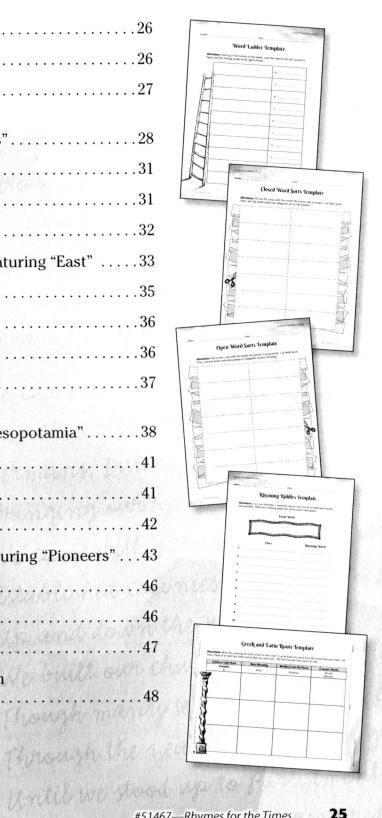

Word Ladders Model Lesson

Standards

- Read closely to determine what the text says explicitly and to make logical inferences from it; cite specific textual evidence when writing or speaking to support conclusions drawn from the text.

- Demonstrate command of the conventions of standard English capitalization, punctuation, and spelling when writing.

Materials

- copies of a verse text for the lesson
- *Word Ladder Template* (page 27)

Procedures

Introducing the Verse Text

- Allow students to read the poem silently.

- Then, read the poem aloud as students follow along. Be sure to model fluent, expressive reading. Have students reread the poem chorally with partners and again as a class.

- Engage in a class discussion about the poem. You may choose to ask questions about the main idea of the poem, discuss and define any unfamiliar words, ask how the poem makes students feel, ask what they think various phrases in the poem mean, and so on.

Vocabulary Strategy Steps

1. Before the lesson, use the *Word Ladder Template* (page 27, wordladders.pdf) to create a word ladder for the words in the poem you are sharing with students. (A Microsoft Word® version of this template is available with the digital resources online.) You can have anywhere from 6 to 12 clues. The template on page 27 has space for 10 clues. There are three additional templates (6, 8, and 12 words) provided as part of the digital resources online. (Also included with the digital downloads are examples of word ladders to help you get started.) Make copies of your completed page for your students.

2. Introduce word ladders and explain how they should be completed. The key aspects of word ladders are that all the words need to be connected in some way and that you start from the bottom and move up the ladder.

3. Distribute the word ladder you created. Have students work in pairs or small groups to complete your word ladder. Provide guidance to students as needed.

4. Many students will enjoy creating their own word ladders. Provide them with copies of the templates and let them create their own ladders using the words from poems or other texts. After students finish creating their word ladders, have them exchange papers with other groups or students and complete them.

Name:_____ Date: _____

Word Ladder Template

Directions: Starting at the bottom of the ladder, read the clues in the left column to figure out the missing words in the right column.

	10. _____
	9. _____
	8. _____
	7. _____
	6. _____
	5. _____
	4. _____
	3. _____
	2. _____
	1. _____

Word Ladder Example Lesson Featuring "Original Thirteen Colonies"

Standards

- Read closely to determine what the text says explicitly and to make logical inferences from it; cite specific textual evidence when writing or speaking to support conclusions drawn from the text.

- Demonstrate command of the conventions of standard English capitalization, punctuation, and spelling when writing.

Materials

- "Original Thirteen Colonies" (page 29)
- *Word Ladder for "Original Thirteen Colonies"* (page 30)

Procedures

Introducing the Verse Text

- Allow students to read "Original Thirteen Colonies" (page 29) silently.

- Then, read the poem aloud as students follow along. Be sure to model fluent, expressive reading. Have students reread the poem chorally with partners and again as a class.

- Engage in a class discussion using the following questions as a guide:

  ✳ The poem says there were many differences among the people who came to the New World. What were some of these differences?

  ✳ What things did these people have in common?

  ✳ According to the poem, what kinds of risks did the colonists take?

Vocabulary Strategy Steps

1. Introduce word ladders and explain how they should be completed.

2. Distribute *Word Ladder for "Original Thirteen Colonies"* (page 30, wordladder_colonies.pdf). Have students complete the ladder either independently or in small groups. Provide guidance to students as needed.

3. Check students' work.

10. free	**5.** line
9. tree	**4.** lice
8. tee	**3.** rice
7. tin	**2.** rise
6. tine (Be prepared; this one is hard!)	**1.** risk

Original Thirteen Colonies

By David L. Harrison

They came, the Dutch,
Swedes, Finns, English,
Quakers, Puritans,
Spanish, French, adventurers
by sea in crowded, pitching ships—
farmers, soldiers, men of trade,
seeking their way,
seeking freedom,
seeking new life in a new world.

Life was harsh,
many died;
many died
but others came,
seeking their way.

Others came and others came
until colonies grew
and many people
with different beliefs,
different customs,
different languages,
governed themselves in peace.

They were the ones
who risked all to become
The United States.

Name:_____ Date:_____

Word Ladder for "Original Thirteen Colonies"

Directions: Starting at the bottom of the ladder, read the clues in the left column to figure out the missing words in the right column.

The colonists risked everything so they could be _____. *(change: first letter)*	10. _____
These grow outside and provide shade on a sunny day. *(change: add one letter)*	9. _____
A golfer hits the ball from a _____. *(change: last two letters)*	8. _____
Metal used in cans *(change: drop one letter)*	7. _____
A prong on a fork *(change: the first letter)*	6. _____
In school, everyone walks down the hallway in a straight _____. *(change: one letter)*	5. _____
These little critters can live in people's hair. *(change: first letter)*	4. _____
You might eat this food as a side dish with your dinner. *(change: one letter)*	3. _____
The sun does this every morning. *(change: last letter)*	2. _____
When the people came to the New World, they knew they were taking a _____.	1. _____

Closed Word Sorts Model Lesson

Standards

- Determine central ideas or themes of a text and analyze their development; summarize the key supporting details and ideas.
- Read closely to determine what the text says explicitly and to make logical inferences from it; cite specific textual evidence when writing or speaking to support conclusions drawn from the text.

Materials

- copies of a verse text for the lesson
- *Closed Word Sorts Template* (page 32)

Procedures

Introducing the Verse Text

- Allow students to read the poem silently.
- Then, read the poem aloud as students follow along. Be sure to model fluent, expressive reading. Have students get in pairs and figure out fun ways to reread the poem chorally together. Allow students time to share their recitations.
- Engage in a class discussion about the poem. You may choose to ask questions about the main idea of the poem, discuss and define any unfamiliar words, ask how the poem makes students feel, ask what they think various phrases in the poem mean, and so on.

Vocabulary Strategy Steps

1. Before the lesson, choose 14 words from the poem. Write these words on the *Closed Word Sorts Template* (page 32, closedsorts.pdf) and distribute copies to students. (A Microsoft Word® version of this template is available with the digital resources online.) Have students cut apart the cards.

2. Briefly discuss the words as a class. Make sure students are familiar with the definitions and meanings.

3. Provide students with a general category. Some category suggestions include number of syllables, parts of speech, location, and time period. Ask students to sort the word cards according to the category you have chosen.

4. Ask students to share their sorts with partners, groups, or the entire class.

5. Have students complete at least two different closed word sorts using categories you have designated.

Name: _____ Date: _____

Closed Word Sorts Template

Directions: Fill out the cards with the words the teacher has provided. Cut them apart. Then, sort the word cards into categories set by the teacher.

Closed Word Sorts
Example Lesson Featuring "East"

 ## Standards

- Determine central ideas or themes of a text and analyze their development; summarize the key supporting details and ideas.

- Read closely to determine what the text says explicitly and to make logical inferences from it; cite specific textual evidence when writing or speaking to support conclusions drawn from the text.

 ## Materials

- "East" (page 34)
- *Closed Word Sorts for "East"* (page 35)

 ## Procedures

Introducing the Verse Text

- Allow students to read "East" (page 34) silently.

- Read the poem aloud as students follow along. Be sure to model fluent, expressive reading. Then, have students get in pairs and figure out fun ways to read the poem chorally together. Allow students time to share their recitations.

- Engage in a class discussion using the following questions as a guide:
  * What does "ring around the lakes" mean?
  * How does the poem prove its case that it is East?
  * In what ways does this poem make East sound like a person?

Vocabulary Strategy Steps

1. Distribute *Closed Word Sorts for "East"* (page 35, closedsorts_east.pdf), and have students cut apart the cards.

2. Briefly discuss the words as a class. Make sure students are familiar with the definitions and meanings.

3. Ask students to sort the words into two categories: words that describe or represent the poem "East" and words that do not describe or represent the poem "East."

> **Represent:** *North, South, Maine, Wisconsin, Tennessee, swamps, sand, lakes, sea, Eastern, mountains*
> **Do Not Represent:** *Canada, Western, Mississippi*

4. Then, ask students to sort the words according to the number of syllables in each word. Follow with a discussion of word meanings and rules for syllabication.

One Syllable:	*North, South, Maine, swamps, sand, sea, lakes*
Two Syllables:	*Eastern, Western, mountains*
Three Syllables:	*Tennessee, Wisconsin, Canada*
Four Syllables:	*Mississippi*

East

By David L. Harrison

We're the eastern states.
Know why?
That old Mississippi
lies somewhere to our west,
so we're East.

Twenty-six of us in all,
North, South, in between,
Maine, Wisconsin, Tennessee,
no matter whatever else we may be,
we're East.

Whether we neighbor Canada,
sit along the beach,
or ring around the Great Lakes,
we're East.

North, South, in between,
mountains, swamps, sand and sea,
no matter whatever else we may be,
that old Mississippi
lies somewhere to our west,
so we're East.

Name:_____   Date: _____

Closed Word Sorts for "East"

Directions: Cut apart the cards. Then, sort the word cards into categories set by the teacher.

North	South
Eastern	Tennessee
Maine	Wisconsin
Canada	Western
mountains	swamps
Mississippi	sand
sea	lakes

Open Word Sorts
Model Lesson

Standards

- Determine central ideas or themes of a text and analyze their development; summarize the key supporting details and ideas.
- Interpret words and phrases as they are used in a text, including determining technical, connotative, and figurative meanings, and analyze how specific word choices shape meaning or tone.

Materials

- copies of the verse text for the lesson
- *Open Word Sorts Template* (page 37)

Procedures

Introducing the Verse Text

- Allow students to read the poem silently.
- Then, read the poem aloud as students follow along. Be sure to model fluent, expressive reading. Have students reread the poem chorally in small groups. Finally, have students record themselves reading the poem so that they can hear how they sound.
- Engage in a class discussion about the poem. You may choose to ask questions about the main idea of the poem, discuss and define any unfamiliar words, ask how the poem makes students feel, ask what they think various phrases in the poem mean, and so on.

Vocabulary Strategy Steps

1. Before the lesson, choose 14 words from the poem. Write these words on the *Open Word Sorts Template* (page 37, opensorts.pdf) and distribute copies to students. (A Microsoft Word® version of this template is available with the digital resources online.) Have students cut apart the cards.

2. Briefly discuss the words as a class. Make sure students are familiar with the definitions and meanings.

3. Allow students to work with partners to sort the words into categories of their own choosing. Challenge students to create at least two different word sorts using the same cards.

4. Ask students to share their sorts with the class without telling what categories they used. As students share their sorts, have the rest of the class guess the categories.

Name:_____ Date: _____

Open Word Sorts Template

Directions: Fill out the cards with the words the teacher has provided. Cut them apart. Then, sort the word cards into groups or categories of your choosing.

Open Word Sorts Example Lesson Featuring "Cradle of Civilization—Mesopotamia"

Standards

- Determine central ideas or themes of a text and analyze their development; summarize the key supporting details and ideas.
- Interpret words and phrases as they are used in a text, including determining technical, connotative, and figurative meanings, and analyze how specific word choices shape meaning or tone.

Materials

- "Cradle of Civilization—Mesopotamia" (page 39)
- *Open Word Sorts for "Cradle of Civilization—Mesopotamia"* (page 40)

Procedures

Introducing the Verse Text

- Allow students to read "Cradle of Civilization—Mesopotamia" (page 39) silently.
- Then, read the poem aloud as students follow along. Be sure to model fluent, expressive reading. Have students reread the poem chorally in small groups. Finally, have students record themselves reading the poem so that they can hear how they sound.
- Engage in a class discussion using the following questions as a guide:
  * Why is Mesopotamia called a "Cradle" in the poem?
  * What effect did being between two rivers have on the land?
  * What do you know about this part of the world today?
  * Why do you think there were so many different professions in ancient Mesopotamia?

Vocabulary Strategy Steps

1. Distribute *Open Word Sorts for "Cradle of Civilization—Mesopotamia"* (page 40, opensorts_mesopotamia.pdf). Have students cut apart the cards.
2. Briefly discuss the words as a class. Make sure students are familiar with the definitions and meanings.
3. Allow students to work with partners to sort the words into categories of their own choosing. Challenge students to create at least two different word sorts using the same cards.
4. Ask students to share their sorts with the class without telling what categories they used. As students share their sorts, have the rest of the class guess the categories.

Cradle of Civilization—Mesopotamia (3100–539 B.C.E.)

By David L. Harrison

Mesopotamia,
how shall we know you,
ancient "land between rivers?"

Between Euphrates
and mighty Tigris—
mountains, deserts, marshes,

Home to fishermen,
herders of goats,
tribesmen, nomads, villagers.

Mesopotamia,
we shall call you,
"Cradle of Civilization."

Home to scholars,
mathematicians,
students of stars and writing.

Some distant day
your history will feed
many differing cultures—

Iraq, Iran,
Syria, Turkey—
the heritage of Mesopotamia.

Name:_____ Date: _____

Open Word Sorts for
"Cradle of Civilization—Mesopotamia"

Directions: Cut apart the cards. Then, sort the word cards into groups or categories of your choosing.

Euphrates	mountains
Tigris	Iraq
herders	desert
Iran	villagers
marshes	Turkey
nomads	Syria
scholars	heritage

Rhyming Riddles Model Lesson

Standards

- Determine central ideas or themes of a text and analyze their development; summarize the key supporting details and ideas.
- Demonstrate command of the conventions of standard English capitalization, punctuation, and spelling when writing.

Materials

- copies of a verse text for the lesson
- *Rhyming Riddles Template* (page 42)

Procedures

Introducing the Verse Text

- Allow students to read the poem silently.
- Then, read the poem aloud as students follow along. Be sure to model fluent, expressive reading. Have students reread the poem chorally in small groups.
- Engage in a class discussion about the poem. You may choose to ask questions about the main idea of the poem, discuss and define any unfamiliar words, ask how the poem makes students feel, ask what they think various phrases in the poem mean, and so on.

Vocabulary Strategy Steps

1. Before the lesson, choose a focus word from the verse text and think of several words that rhyme with it. Fill out the *Rhyming Riddles Template* (page 42, rhymingriddles.pdf) with clues to indicate the words that rhyme with the selected word. (A Microsoft Word® version of this template is available with the digital resources online.) Make copies of the page for students.

2. Choose a different focus word from the verse text that has several rhyming words. You will be using this word as an example to show students how to complete a rhyming riddle. Discuss its meaning and why it is important in the verse text. As a class, brainstorm several words that rhyme with the chosen word. Provide examples of homophones that rhyme with the focus word when possible.

3. Distribute your version of the *Rhyming Riddles Template*. Allow students to work independently or with partners to read through the clues and write the rhyming words.

4. When students finish, discuss the answers. Be sure to review correct spelling.

5. If time allows, have students create their own rhyming riddles using blank copies of the template.

Name:_____   Date: _____

Rhyming Riddles Template

Directions: Each clue describes a word that rhymes with the focus word your teacher has provided. Write each rhyming word next to the correct description.

Focus Word

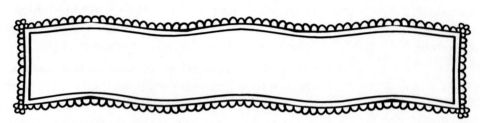

Clues   ### Rhyming Words

1. _____   _____

2. _____   _____

3. _____   _____

4. _____   _____

5. _____   _____

6. _____   _____

7. _____   _____

8. _____   _____

9. _____   _____

10. _____   _____

Rhyming Riddles
Example Lesson Featuring "Pioneers"

Standards

- Determine central ideas or themes of a text and analyze their development; summarize the key supporting details and ideas.
- Demonstrate command of the conventions of standard English capitalization, punctuation, and spelling when writing.

Materials

- "Pioneers" (page 44)
- *Rhyming Riddles for "Pioneers"* (page 45)

Procedures

Introducing the Verse Text

- Allow students to read "Pioneers" (page 44) silently.
- Then, read the poem aloud as students follow along. Be sure to model fluent, expressive reading. Have students reread the poem chorally in small groups.
- Engage in a class discussion using the following questions as a guide:
  - ✷ What types of hardships did pioneers face?
  - ✷ If the trip was so difficult, why do you think so many people moved west?
  - ✷ Do you think you would have liked being a pioneer? Why or why not?

Vocabulary Strategy Steps

1. Call students' attention to the focus word *trail* in the verse text. Discuss its meaning and why it is important in the poem. As a class, brainstorm several words that rhyme with *trail*. Point out rhyming homophones also (e.g., *pail* and *pale*).

2. Distribute *Rhyming Riddles for "Pioneers"* (page 45, rhymingriddles_pioneers.pdf). Students should work independently or with partners.

3. When students are finished, discuss the answers together using the list below. Be sure to review correct spelling.

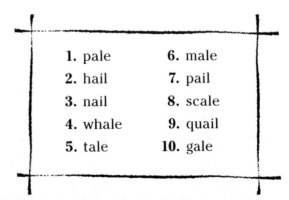

1. pale	6. male
2. hail	7. pail
3. nail	8. scale
4. whale	9. quail
5. tale	10. gale

4. If time allows, have students create their own rhyming riddles using the *Rhyming Riddles Template* (page 42).

Pioneers

By David L. Harrison

No interstates,
no highways,
no roads, paved or graveled.
Only trails toward the westward sun,
scarred and rutted by iron clad wheels
of wagons creaking under loads
of what families needed along the way
and at the end of their journey.

No room for passengers
except the weak and ill
amid the stores of food,
dishes, clothing, furniture,
tools, bedding . . .

Lucky ones rode horse or mule,
others walked by their wagon,
struggling ten miles a day,
month after weary month
for half a year through heat,
flooded rivers, hostile territory.

Yet they came,
and still they came,
determined folks determined
to start anew in a new world.
They peopled the west,
ensured the future
of young America.

Name:_____ Date: _____

Rhyming Riddles for "Pioneers"

Directions: Each clue describes a word that rhymes with *trail*. Write each rhyming word next to the correct clue.

Focus Word

trail

Clues   Rhyming Words

1. to not have much color   _____

2. icy precipitation   _____

3. what a hammer hits   _____

4. a huge water mammal   _____

5. a made-up story   _____

6. another word for a man or a boy   _____

7. similar to a bucket   _____

8. measures weight   _____

9. a small bird   _____

10. big gust of wind   _____

Greek and Latin Roots Model Lesson

 ## Standards

- Read closely to determine what the text says explicitly and to make logical inferences from it; cite specific textual evidence when writing or speaking to support conclusions drawn from the text.

- Determine or clarify the meaning of unknown and multiple-meaning words and phrases by using context clues, analyzing meaningful word parts, and consulting general and specialized reference materials, as appropriate.

 ## Materials

- copies of a verse text for the lesson
- *Greek and Latin Roots Template* (page 47)

 ## Procedures

Introducing the Verse Text

- Allow students to read the poem silently.

- Then, read the poem aloud as students follow along. Be sure to model fluent, expressive reading. Have students reread the poem carefully and circle any words they think are especially important. As they read chorally with partners, they should put special emphasis on those words.

- Engage in a class discussion about the poem. You may choose to ask questions about the main idea of the poem, discuss and define any unfamiliar words, ask how the poem makes students feel, ask what they think various phrases in the poem mean, and so on.

Vocabulary Strategy Steps

1. Before the lesson, find two to three words in the verse text with Greek or Latin roots. Think about the meanings of the roots and how they affect the meanings of the words. Share this information with your students.

2. Write the chosen word roots in the left column of the *Greek and Latin Roots Template* (page 47, greeklatin.pdf). Make copies of this page for your students. (A Microsoft Word® version of this template is available with the digital resources online.)

3. As you look at the verse text together, assist students in finding and defining Greek or Latin roots from the text. Discuss word meanings and the clues the roots give.

4. Distribute copies of the *Greek and Latin Roots Template* from Step 2.

5. Students may work independently or in small groups to define the given roots and brainstorm additional words.

Additional examples of Greek and Latin roots from other poems in this book include:

Poem	Root	Word(s) from Poem	Example Words
"New York" (page 93)	*migra*	immigrants	emigrate; migratory
"Puritan Woman" (page 121)	*uni*	uniform	unicorn; unique

Name: _____ Date: _____

Greek and Latin Roots Template

Directions: Write the meaning for each Greek or Latin root. Find at least one word from the poem that uses each root. Then, think of at least two other words that use each root. The first one has been done for you.

Greek or Latin Root	Root Meaning	Word(s) from the Poem	Example Words
Example *lit*	letter	literature	literacy illiterate

Greek and Latin Roots
Example Lesson Featuring "Athens—Greece"

 ## Standards

- Read closely to determine what the text says explicitly and to make logical inferences from it; cite specific textual evidence when writing or speaking to support conclusions drawn from the text.

- Determine or clarify the meaning of unknown and multiple-meaning words and phrases by using context clues, analyzing meaningful word parts, and consulting general and specialized reference materials, as appropriate.

 ## Materials

- "Athens—Greece" (page 49)
- *Greek and Latin Roots for "Athens—Greece"* (page 50)

 ## Procedures

Introducing the Verse Text

- Allow students to read "Athens—Greece" (page 49) silently.

- Then, read the poem aloud as students follow along. Be sure to model fluent, expressive reading. Have students reread the poem carefully and circle any words they think are especially important. As they read chorally with partners, they should put special emphasis on those words.

- Engage in a class discussion using the following questions as a guide:

  ✸ What is the Parthenon? Why was it built?

  ✸ Why are Socrates, Plato, and Aristotle significant?

  ✸ How did ancient Greece influence the Western World?

Vocabulary Strategy Steps

1. Call students' attention to words with Greek and Latin roots in the poem. Examples include *patron*, *literature*, *philosophy*, and *democracy*. (Additional examples from other poems in this book are provided on page 46.) Discuss word meanings and what clues the roots give to the meanings of the whole words.

2. Allow students time to find other words in the poem with Greek or Latin roots. Discuss what each root might mean based on the word's definition.

3. Distribute *Greek and Latin Roots for "Athens—Greece"* (page 50, greeklatin_athens.pdf). Allow students to complete the activity independently or in small groups.

4. Check the answers together. Encourage students to think of other Greek and Latin roots.

patr	father	patron	patriarch; patriot
dem	people	democracy	Democrat; epidemic
phil	love	philosophy	philanthropy; bibliophile

Athens—Greece
(479-323 B.C.E.)

By David L. Harrison

And during that golden age
they built the Parthenon,
and Athens,
mighty Athens,
was in its glory.

They built it all of marble
for their patron goddess Athena,
goddess of wisdom, justice, war,
who was born, they said,
full grown out of Zeus's head.

And during that golden age,
Socrates taught Plato
and Plato taught Aristotle.

And Athens,
mighty Athens,
produced art and literature,
philosophy, democracy,
influenced all the Western World
like few before.

Name: _____ Date: _____

Greek and Latin Roots for "Athens—Greece"

Directions: Write a definition for each Greek or Latin root. Find at least one word from the poem that uses each root. Then, think of at least two other words that use each root. The first one has been done for you.

Greek or Latin Root	Root Meaning	Word(s) from the Poem	Other Words
Example *lit*	letter	literature	literacy illiterate
patr			
dem			
phil			

Strategies for Word Play

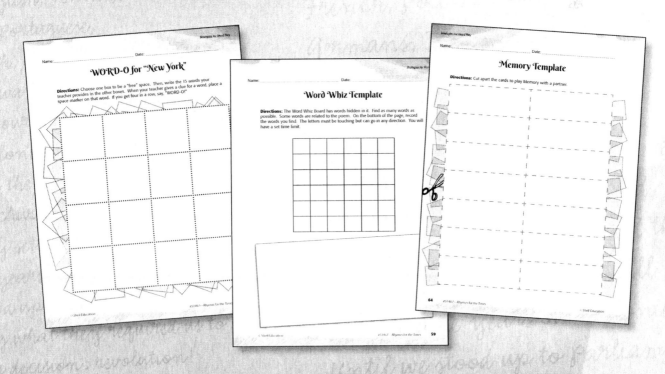

WORD-O
Model Lesson

 ## Standards

- Interpret words and phrases as they are used in a text, including determining technical, connotative, and figurative meanings, and analyze how specific word choices shape meaning or tone.

- Read closely to determine what the text says explicitly and to make logical inferences from it; cite specific textual evidence when writing or speaking to support conclusions drawn from the text.

 ## Materials

- copies of a verse text for the lesson
- slips of paper
- *WORD-O Template* (page 53)
- coins or chips to use as space markers

 ## Procedures

Introducing the Verse Text

- Allow students to read the poem silently.

- Then, read the poem aloud as students follow along. Be sure to model fluent, expressive reading. Have students practice reading the poem orally for a performance. Set up a day when the students can visit other classes and share the poem. (You may want to choose younger students so that your students are more comfortable than they might be with their peers.)

- Engage in a class discussion about the poem. You may choose to ask questions about the main idea of the poem, discuss and define any unfamiliar words, ask how the poem makes students feel, ask what they think various phrases in the poem mean, and so on.

Word Play Strategy Steps

1. Before the lesson, choose 15 to 20 words from the poem or words related to its topic. Write these words on small slips of paper for you to use during the activity.

2. Display your chosen words for students.

3. Distribute copies of the *WORD-O Template* (page 53, wordo.pdf) to students. (A Microsoft Word® version of this template is available with the digital resources online.) Provide students with coins, chips, or similar objects as space markers. Have each student select one space to be a "free" space. Then, have students add the selected words to their boards in any order.

4. Have students place space markers on their free spaces. Pull your words (on slips of paper) out of a hat or a box. Give a clue for each word. You can define the word, give a synonym or an antonym for it, or even state a sentence with the word missing from it.

5. Students should place space markers on words when they hear their clues. When students get four words in a row, diagonally, or running up and down, they should say, "WORD-O!"

Name:_____ Date: _____

WORD-O Template

Directions: Choose one box to be a "free" space. Then, write the 15 words your teacher provides in the other boxes. When your teacher gives a clue for a word, place a space marker on that word. If you get four in a row, say, "WORD-O!"

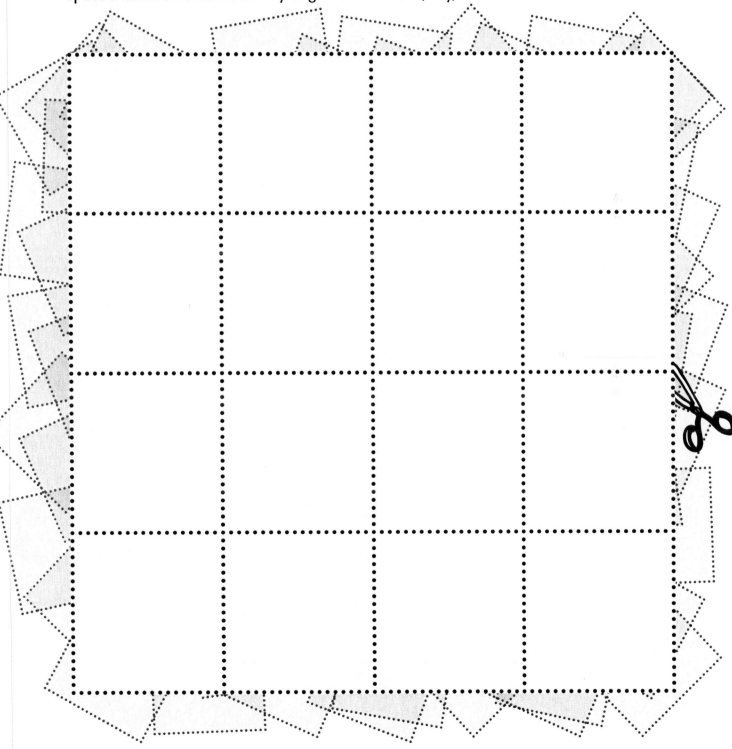

WORD-O
Example Lesson Featuring "New York"

Standards

- Interpret words and phrases as they are used in a text, including determining technical, connotative, and figurative meanings, and analyze how specific word choices shape meaning or tone.

- Read closely to determine what the text says explicitly and to make logical inferences from it; cite specific textual evidence when writing or speaking to support conclusions drawn from the text.

Materials

- "New York" (page 56)
- *WORD-O Words and Clues* for *"New York"* (page 55)
- *WORD-O for "New York"* (page 57)
- coins or chips to use as space markers

Procedures

Introducing the Verse Text

- Allow students to read "New York" (page 56) silently.

- Then, read the poem aloud as students follow along. Be sure to model fluent, expressive reading. Have students practice reading the poem orally for a performance. Set up a day when the students can visit other classes and share the poem. (You may want to choose younger students so that your students are more comfortable than they might be with their peers.)

- Engage in a class discussion using the following questions as a guide:

  * What does the poem mean when it says, "Americans / trace their roots / to weary travelers"?

  * Why would New York say that "no one's more American than I"?

  * According to the poem, why is New York important?

Word Play Strategy Steps

1. Before the lesson, cut apart the clues from page 55 to use during the activity. Place them in a hat or a box.

2. Write the words at the top of page 55 on the board for the class. This page is also included with the digital resources online (wordo_nycards.pdf).

3. Distribute sets of *WORD-O for "New York"* (page 57, wordo_ny.pdf) to individual students. Provide students with coins, chips, or similar objects as *WORD-O* space markers. Have each student select one space to be a "free" space. Then, have students add the words to the remaining boxes in any order.

4. Have students place space markers on their free spaces. Pull the words out of the hat or box. Read the clue for each word.

5. Students should place space markers on words when they hear their clues. When students get four words in a row, diagonally, or running up and down, they should say, "WORD-O!"

WORD-O Words and Clues for "New York"

Words to Display

America	country	duke	emigrate
English	freedom	immigrants	million
New York	proud	roots	shore
Statue of Liberty	trace	travelers	weary

Clues

America: United States	**country:** the land of a person's birth, residence, or citizenship	**duke:** a nobleman from England	**emigrate:** when someone leaves a country to live somewhere else
English: people of England	**freedom:** to have liberty and independence	**immigrants:** people who go to another country to live	**million:** large number
New York: state in the eastern United States where many immigrants first arrived	**proud:** having self-respect	**roots:** established place to live	**shore:** the coastline
Statue of Liberty: famous landmark that let immigrants know they had made it to America	**trace:** to follow or track	**travelers:** voyagers	**weary:** tired, exhausted

New York

By David L. Harrison

We are a country of immigrants
and I am the state where many
first saw this great land.

One hundred million Americans
trace their roots
to weary travelers
just off boats and weeks at sea
who stood in lines as long as it took
to step at last on freedom's shore,
my shore.

I was named for an English duke,
but no one's more American than I.
I'm proud to be New York.

Name:_____ Date: _____

WORD-O for "New York"

Directions: Choose one box to be a "free" space. Then, write the 15 words your teacher provides in the other boxes. When your teacher gives a clue for a word, place a space marker on that word. If you get four in a row, say, "WORD-O!"

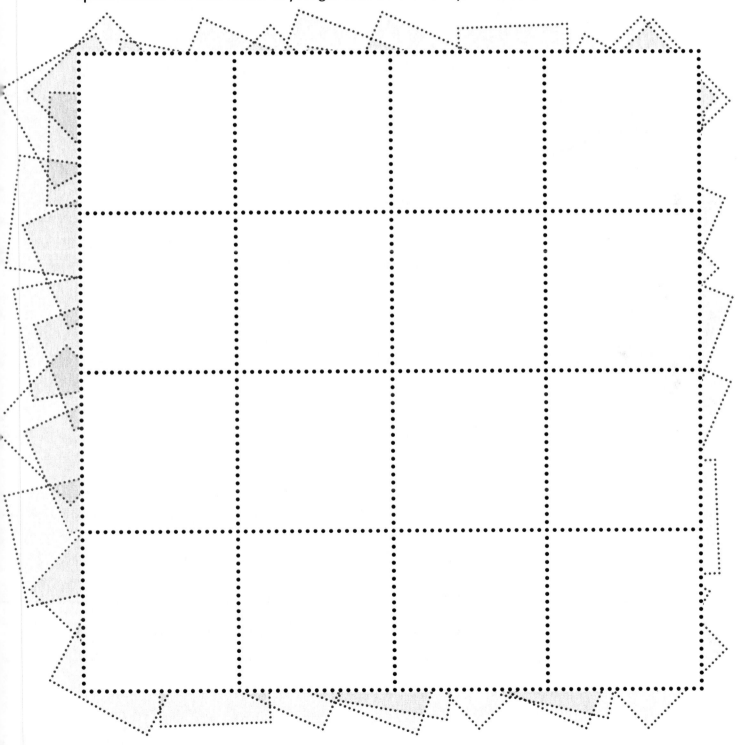

Word Whiz Model Lesson

Standards

- Determine central ideas or themes of a text and analyze their development; summarize the key supporting details and ideas.
- Read closely to determine what the text says explicitly and to make logical inferences from it; cite specific textual evidence when writing or speaking to support conclusions drawn from the text.

Materials

- copies of a verse text for the lesson
- *Word Whiz Template* (page 59)

Procedures

Introducing the Verse Text

- Allow students to read the poem silently.
- Then, read the poem aloud as students follow along. Be sure to model fluent, expressive reading. Have students divide the poem into parts and reread it with partners.
- Engage in a class discussion about the poem. You may choose to ask questions about the main idea of the poem, discuss and define any unfamiliar words, ask how the poem makes students feel, ask what they think various phrases in the poem mean, and so on.

Word Play Strategy Steps

1. Before the lesson, create a Word Whiz board for the verse text. Fill in the *Word Whiz Template* (page 59, wordwhiz.pdf) with four to six words specific to the poem or its content. (A Microsoft Word® version of this template is available with the digital resources online.) The word should be "hidden" among other letters on the Word Whiz board. Make sure other words that are not content-specific can also be found.

2. Distribute copies of your Word Whiz board to students. You may choose to have them play in groups or in pairs.

3. Explain that to make a word, letters must be touching vertically, horizontally, or diagonally, and the letters must be in order of sequence. The words can go in any direction—left, right, up, down—and can change directions, but the letters in sequence must be touching. Give students at least five minutes to find as many words as possible.

4. The scoring is as follows: two points for a two-letter word, three points for three-letter word, and so on. Award 10 points for each of the content-specific words you chose. You can decide if you want to give students these words in advance. The student(s) with the most points wins!

Name:_____ Date: _____

Word Whiz Template

Directions: The Word Whiz Board has words hidden in it. Find as many words as possible. Some words are related to the poem. On the bottom of the page, record the words you find. The letters must be touching but can go in any direction. You will have a set time limit.

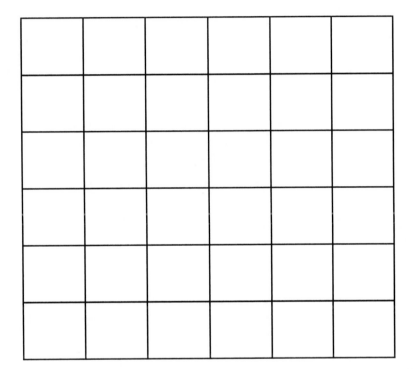

Word Whiz
Example Lesson Featuring "North Carolina"

Standards

- Determine central ideas or themes of a text and analyze their development; summarize the key supporting details and ideas.

- Read closely to determine what the text says explicitly and to make logical inferences from it; cite specific textual evidence when writing or speaking to support conclusions drawn from the text.

Materials

- "North Carolina" (page 61)

- *Word Whiz for "North Carolina"* (page 62)

Procedures

Introducing the Verse Text

- Allow students to read "North Carolina" (page 61) silently.

- Then, read the poem aloud as students follow along. Be sure to model fluent, expressive reading. Have students divide the poem into parts and reread it with partners.

- Engage in a class discussion using the following questions as a guide:

  ✳ Based on the poem, what kinds of things would you expect to see in North Carolina?

  ✳ Why would history be tinted "through mists of time"?

  ✳ What does the phrase "where lost ships sleep" mean in the poem? How do you know?

Word Play Strategy Steps

1. Distribute *Word Whiz for "North Carolina"* (page 62, wordwhiz_northcarolina.pdf) to students. You may choose to have them work in groups or in pairs.

2. Explain that to make a word, letters must be touching vertically, horizontally, or diagonally, and the letters must be in order of sequence. The words can go in any direction—left, right, up, down—and can change directions, but the letters in sequence must be touching. Give students at least five minutes to find as many words as possible.

3. The scoring is as follows: two points for a two-letter word, three points for a three-letter word, and so on. Award 10 points for each of these content-specific words: *time*, *basins*, *Indian*, *Spanish*, and *mist*. You can choose if you want to give students these words in advance. The student(s) with the most points wins!

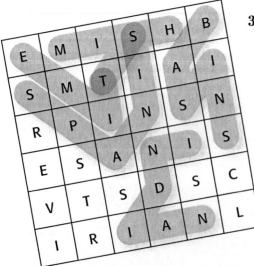

North Carolina

By David L. Harrison

From watery graves,
off Cape Hatteras
where lost ships sleep
to Mount Mitchell's craggy face
I offer you history tinted
through mists of time—
Indians who called this land their home,
Spanish conquistadors,
English settlers who risked all
to make this land theirs too.

I offer you river basins, rich soil
where melons, soybeans, cotton grow.

A modern state with ancient roots,
I offer you North Carolina.

Name:_____   Date: _____

Word Whiz for "North Carolina"

Directions: The Word Whiz Board has words hidden in it. Find as many words as possible. Some words are related to the poem. On the bottom of the page, record the words you find. The letters must be touching but can go in any direction. You will have a set time limit.

E	M	I	S	H	B
S	M	T	I	A	I
R	P	I	N	S	N
E	S	A	N	I	S
V	T	S	D	S	C
I	R	I	A	N	L

Memory Model Lesson

Standards

- Acquire and use accurately a range of general academic and domain-specific words and phrases sufficient for reading, writing, speaking, and listening at the college and career readiness level; demonstrate independence in gathering vocabulary knowledge when encountering an unknown term important to comprehension or expression.
- Read closely to determine what the text says explicitly and to make logical inferences from it; cite specific textual evidence when writing or speaking to support conclusions drawn from the text.

Materials

- copies of a verse text for the lesson
- *Memory Template* (page 64)

Procedures

Introducing the Verse Text

- Have students read the poem silently multiple times. Then, have them pair up with partners and read the poem to each other. Did they both recite it the same way with the same emphases and fluency? Or did they read it differently?
- After discussing how the students read the poem, read the poem aloud as students follow along. Be sure to model fluent, expressive reading.
- Engage in a class discussion about the poem. You may choose to ask questions about the main idea of the poem, discuss and define any unfamiliar words, ask how the poem makes students feel, ask what they think various phrases in the poem mean, and so on.

Word Play Strategy Steps

1. Before the lesson, choose seven important words from the verse text. Fill out the *Memory Template* (page 64, memory.pdf) using the words and their definitions or descriptions. (A Microsoft Word® version of this template is available with the digital resources online.) Make copies of your Memory board for students.

2. Distribute copies of your *Memory Template* to pairs of students. Students will cut apart the cards and arrange them facedown on a flat surface.

3. Explain how to play Memory. The first player turns over two cards and tries to make a match between a word and its definition/description. If a match is made, the player takes another turn. If no match is made, the player returns the cards to the original positions. Then, it is the other player's turn.

4. Continue playing until all cards have been matched. In each pair of students, the player with the most matches wins.

Name:_____ Date:_____

Memory Template

Directions: Cut apart the cards to play Memory with a partner.

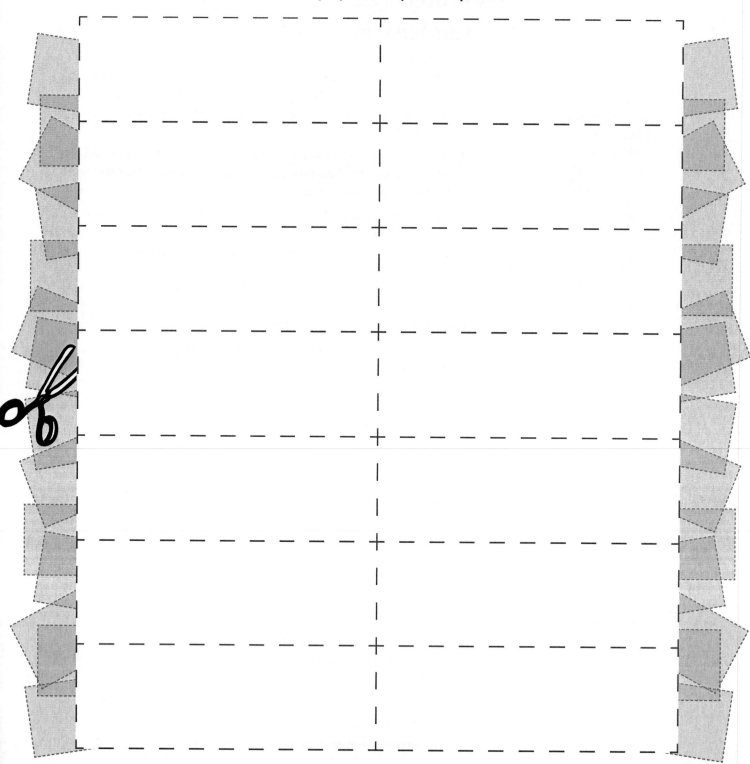

Memory Example Lesson featuring "The Farmer—Neolithic"

 ## Standards

- Acquire and use accurately a range of general academic and domain-specific words and phrases sufficient for reading, writing, speaking, and listening; demonstrate independence in gathering vocabulary knowledge when encountering an unknown term important to comprehension or expression.

- Read closely to determine what the text says explicitly and to make logical inferences from it; cite specific textual evidence when writing or speaking to support conclusions drawn from the text.

 ## Materials

- "The Farmer—Neolithic" (page 66)
- *Memory for "The Farmer—Neolithic"* (page 67)

 ## Procedures

Introducing the Verse Text

- Have students read "The Farmer—Neolithic" (page 66) silently multiple times. Then, have them pair up with partners and read the poem to each other. Did they both recite it the same way with the same emphases and fluency? Or did they read it differently?

- After discussing how the students read the poem, read the poem aloud as students follow along. Be sure to model fluent, expressive reading.

- Engage in a class discussion using the following questions as a guide:

  ✳ What does the poem mean by "settling down"?

  ✳ According to the poem, what were the advantages of settling down?

  ✳ How did planting and harvesting change the lives of all who followed?

Word Play Strategy Steps

1. Distribute *Memory for "The Farmer—Neolithic"* (page 67, memory_farmer.pdf) to pairs of students. Students should cut apart the cards and arrange them facedown on a flat surface.

2. Explain how to play Memory. The first player turns over two cards and tries to make a match between a word and its definition. If a match is made, the player takes another turn. If no match is made, the player returns the cards to the original positions. Then, it is the other player's turn.

3. Continue playing until all cards have been matched. For each pair, the player with the most matches wins.

Matches are as follows:

banding—grouping together
migrating—moving from one area to another
herds—large groups of animals kept together
spears—weapons with a pointed tip used for thrusting
fashioned—used materials to make something
brittle—hard, but breaks easily
reeds—tall, thin grasses that grow in water or marshes

The Farmer—Neolithic (10,000–2000 B.C.E.)

By David L. Harrison

There came a time 12,000 years ago
when people started settling down, keeping
dogs, raising sheep and goats, planting
wheat, gathering wild crops, banding

Together in settled camps instead of following
migrating herds hunting meat with spears
and sharp points fashioned from brittle stone.

Farming gave them time to make pots,
weave baskets from reeds, bark, leather,
improve clothing, invent tools, art.

There came a time 12,000 years ago
when planting and harvesting small grains of wheat
forever changed the lives of all who followed.

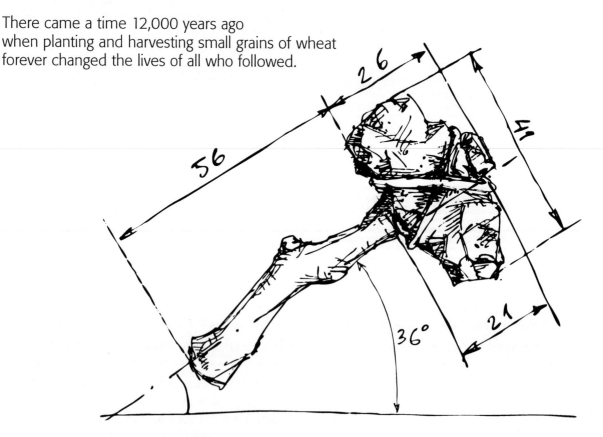

Name:_____ Date:_____

Memory for "The Farmer—Neolithic"

Directions: Cut apart the cards to play Memory with a partner.

banding	grouping together
migrating	moving from one area to another
herds	large groups of animals kept together
spears	weapons with a pointed tip used for thrusting
fashioned	used materials to make something
brittle	hard, but breaks easily
reeds	tall, thin grasses that grow in water or marshes

Content-Based Strategies

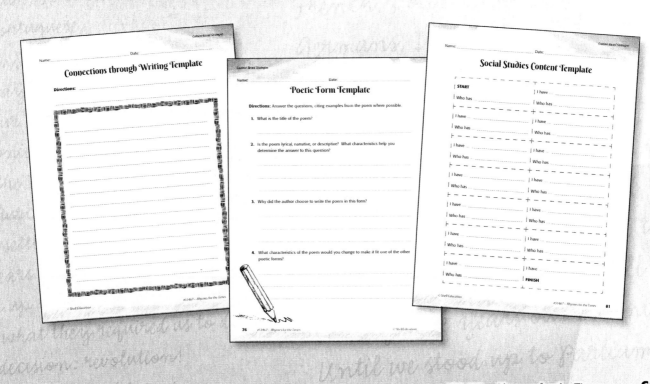

Connections through Writing Model Lesson

 ## Standards

- Draw evidence from literary or informational texts to support analysis, reflection, and research.
- Read closely to determine what the text says explicitly and to make logical inferences from it; cite specific textual evidence when writing or speaking to support conclusions drawn from the text.

 ## Materials

- copies of a verse text for the lesson
- *Connections through Writing Template* (page 71)

 ## Procedures

Introducing the Verse Text

- Allow students to read the poem silently.
- Then, read the poem aloud as students follow along. Be sure to model fluent, expressive reading. Have students reread the poem with partners, alternating stanzas and then switching who begins reading so that each student reads all stanzas.
- Engage in a class discussion about the poem. You may choose to ask questions about the main idea of the poem, discuss and define any unfamiliar words, ask how the poem makes students feel, ask what they think various phrases in the poem mean, and so on.

Content-Based Strategy Steps

1. Before the lesson, decide on a writing prompt for the students. Include the directions for the prompt on the *Connections through Writing Template* (page 71, writing.pdf). (Microsoft Word® versions of this and two additional writing templates are available with the digital resources online.) General prompts and ideas include an expository essay, a letter to a historical figure, a poem, a historical narrative, or a journal entry of a historical figure.

2. Distribute copies of the *Connections through Writing Template* with the prompt filled in to students. Emphasize the steps of the writing process and encourage creativity. Have students brainstorm ideas for the prompt on their own or with partners.

3. If time permits, have students add illustrations to go with their written responses.

4. Ask volunteers to share their work with the class.

Name:_____ Date: _____

Connections through Writing Template

Directions: _____

_____

_____

_____

_____

_____

_____

_____

_____

_____

_____

_____

_____

Connections through Writing Example Lesson Featuring "General George Washington"

 ## Standards

- Draw evidence from literary or informational texts to support analysis, reflection, and research.
- Read closely to determine what the text says explicitly and to make logical inferences from it; cite specific textual evidence when writing or speaking to support conclusions drawn from the text.

 ## Materials

- "General George Washington" (page 73)
- *Connections through Writing for "General George Washington"* (page 74)

 ## Procedures

Introducing the Verse Text

- Allow students to read "General George Washington" (page 73) silently.
- Then, read the poem aloud as students follow along. Be sure to model fluent, expressive reading. Have students reread the poem with partners. Have them read together so that the first student reads one stanza and the other student reads the next stanza.
- Engage in a class discussion using the following questions as a guide:
  * What difficulties did the soldiers face?
  * Why do you think Congress did not respond to the plight of the soldiers?
  * What does "But victory comes at a terrible price" mean?

Content-Based Strategy Steps

1. Distribute *Connections through Writing for "General George Washington"* (page 74, writing_washington.pdf).
2. Discuss the soldiers' feelings and how George Washington wants them to feel. Emphasize the steps of the writing process and encourage creativity. Have students brainstorm on their own or with partners how Washington could help his soldiers.
3. Allow students time to complete their letters. Remind them of the various parts of a friendly letter (e.g., salutation, body, closing). If time permits, have students add illustrations to go with their written responses.
4. Ask volunteers to share their work with the class.

General George Washington

By David L. Harrison

I saw a lad this morning,
no different, really,
from thousands of others,
shivering over a meager fire,
attempting to warm his feet
where they stuck through
holes in his boots.

Pale, gaunt as a starving wolf,
he looked tempted
to boil his boots for supper,
nor would he be the first.

Wherever I go it's the same,
exhausted men perishing in the cold,
wasting away from hunger.
Yet there are those in Congress
who do not see
the plight of these men,
their desperate need for warm clothes,
boots, food . . .

We would lose this war
but for these brave fighters.
They look to me to lead them to victory.
I can do no less.
I tell them, in spite of all odds,
we shall prevail.

I must, and I do believe,
that we shall persevere.
But victory comes at a terrible price.
It cannot come too soon!

Name:_____ Date: _____

Connections through Writing for "General George Washington"

Directions: Write a letter from General George Washington to inspire and comfort his soldiers. Be sure to include all parts of a friendly letter.

Poetic Form Model Lesson

Standards

- Interpret words and phrases as they are used in a text, including determining technical, connotative, and figurative meanings, and analyze how specific word choices shape meaning or tone.
- Read closely to determine what the text says explicitly and to make logical inferences from it; cite specific textual evidence when writing or speaking to support conclusions drawn from the text.

Materials

- copy of a verse text for the lesson
- *Poetic Form Template* (page 76)

Procedures

Introducing the Verse Text

- Allow students to read the poem silently.
- Then, read the poem aloud as students follow along. Be sure to model fluent, expressive reading. Have students record themselves reading the poem chorally with partners. Allow students time to listen to their recordings and redo them if they wish to improve their fluency.
- Engage in a class discussion about the poem. You may choose to ask questions about the main idea of the poem, discuss and define any unfamiliar words, ask how the poem makes students feel, ask what they think various phrases in the poem mean, and so on.

Content-Based Strategy Steps

1. Review the following poetic forms: lyrical poetry (strong feelings, one speaker), narrative poetry (tells a story, has a plot), descriptive poetry (describes the world, uses imagery). More information about these poetic forms is included with the digital resources online (guidelines.pdf). (These specific poetic forms were chosen because they match the 60 poems in this book. If you are using other forms of poetry, introduce those forms to students.)

2. Ask students to share their thoughts on the poem. Encourage them to quote specific lines to support their opinions. Be sure to stress that poems are open to interpretation and there is not necessarily one correct answer.

3. Distribute copies of the *Poetic Form Template* (page 76, poeticform.pdf). (A Microsoft Word® version of this template is available with the digital resources online. You can use the digital copy of this template to change the questions as necessary to better meet your teaching goals.) Students can work individually or with partners. Provide students with enough time to complete the activity.

Name:_____ Date: _____

Poetic Form Template

Directions: Answer the questions, citing examples from the poem where possible.

1. What is the title of the poem?

_____

2. Is the poem lyrical, narrative, or descriptive? What characteristics help you determine the answer to this question?

_____

_____

_____

3. Why did the author choose to write the poem in this form?

_____

_____

_____

4. What characteristics of the poem would you change to make it fit one of the other poetic forms?

_____

_____

_____

Poetic Form
Example Lesson Featuring "Julius Caesar—Rome"

 ## Standards

- Interpret words and phrases as they are used in a text, including determining technical, connotative, and figurative meanings, and analyze how specific word choices shape meaning or tone.

- Read closely to determine what the text says explicitly and to make logical inferences from it; cite specific textual evidence when writing or speaking to support conclusions drawn from the text.

 ## Materials

- "Julius Caesar—Rome" (page 78)
- *Poetic Form for "Julius Caesar—Rome"* (page 79)

 ## Procedures

Introducing the Verse Text

- Allow students to read "Julius Caesar—Rome" (page 78) silently.

- Then, read the poem aloud as students follow along. Be sure to model fluent, expressive reading. Have students record themselves reading the poem chorally with partners. Allow students time to listen to their recordings and redo them if they wish to make them sound more fluent.

- Engage in a class discussion using the following questions as a guide:

  ✱ Why didn't Julius Caesar like Rome?

  ✱ What advantages could there have been to living in Rome?

  ✱ Do you think you would have enjoyed living in Caesar's Rome? Why or why not?

Content-Based Strategy Steps

1. Review the following poetic forms: lyrical poetry (strong feelings, one speaker), narrative poetry (tells a story, has a plot), descriptive poetry (describes the world, uses imagery). More information about these poetic forms is included with the digital resources online (guidelines.pdf). (These specific poetic forms were chosen because they match the 60 poems in this book. If you are using other forms of poetry, introduce those forms to students.)

2. Ask students to share their thoughts on the poem. Encourage them to quote specific lines that support their opinions. Be sure to stress that poems are open to interpretation and there is not necessarily one correct answer.

3. Distribute *Poetic Form for "Julius Caesar—Rome"* (page 79, poeticform_caesar.pdf). Students can work individually or with partners. Provide students with enough time to complete the activity.

Julius Caesar—Rome (46–44 B.C.E.)

By David L. Harrison

Caesar himself,
so it was said,
hated the ruckus—
    chariots rattling stony streets,
    dogs yapping, screaming boys,
    vendors shouting, crowded shops,
    roaring hubbub, thrumming noise—
"Enough!"

Caesar might have said—
    pounding hoof beats, beggars' cries,
    bleating animals, shrieks, squeals,
    cracking whips, roaring crowds,
    warlike groaning iron wheels—

"I cannot think!"
    All was jangle, throb, and clamor,
    Clatter, chatter, clang, and clop.
    Caesar must have held his head
    and longed to make the noises stop.

The biggest city on the earth,
a million people called it home.
"It's noisy here," said Caesar.
It was Rome!

Name:_____ Date: _____

Poetic Form for "Julius Caesar—Rome"

Directions: Answer the questions, citing examples from the poem where possible.

1. What is the title of the poem?

_____

2. Is the poem lyrical, narrative, or descriptive? What characteristics help you determine the answer to this question?

_____

_____

_____

3. Why did the author choose to write the poem in this form?

_____

_____

_____

4. What characteristics of the poem would you change to make it fit one of the other poetic forms?

_____

_____

_____

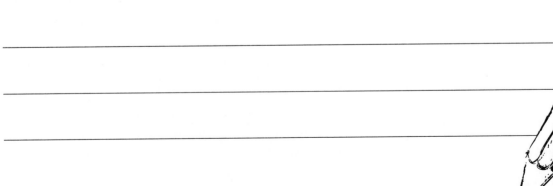

Social Studies Content Model Lesson

Standards

- Acquire and use accurately a range of general academic and domain-specific words and phrases sufficient for reading, writing, speaking, and listening at the college and career readiness level; demonstrate independence in gathering vocabulary knowledge when encountering an unknown term important to comprehension or expression.
- Determine central ideas or themes of a text and analyze their development; summarize the key supporting details and ideas.

Materials

- copies of a verse text for the lesson
- *Social Studies Content Template* (page 81)

Procedures

Introducing the Verse Text

- Allow students to read the poem silently.
- Then, read the poem aloud as students follow along. Be sure to model fluent, expressive reading. Have students reread the poem chorally with partners and again as a class.
- Engage in a class discussion about the poem. You may choose to ask questions about the main idea of the poem, discuss and define any unfamiliar words, ask how the poem makes students feel, ask what they think various phrases in the poem mean, and so on.

Content-Based Strategy Steps

1. Before the lesson, choose 12 vocabulary words, historical figures, or phrases that are important to the verse text's topic. Fill in the "I have . . . . Who has . . . ?" activity cards on the *Social Studies Content Template* (page 81, socialstudies.pdf). (A Microsoft Word® version of this template is available with the digital resources online.) Each card will have the answer to a previous question and will ask a new question to keep the game going. Cut apart the cards.

2. Distribute a card to each student in your class. Depending on the number of students, you may choose to play with small groups, play multiple times, or have students team up with partners. Another option is to make multiple copies of the template to create more cards.

3. Begin the game by having the student with the "START" card read the card aloud. Then, the student with the card that answers the question reads his or her card aloud. For example, *START: Who has the leader of ancient Egypt?* The next student would then read, *I have pharaoh. Who has the famous river in Egypt?* Students continue the game until they have reached the "FINISH" card. Offer clues from the verse text if students need assistance with the answers.

Name: _____ Date: _____

Social Studies Content Template

START

Who has … _____

I have … _____

Who has … _____

I have … _____

Who has … _____

I have … _____

Who has … _____

I have … _____

Who has … _____

I have … _____

Who has … _____

I have … _____

Who has … _____

I have … _____

Who has … _____

I have … _____

Who has … _____

I have … _____

Who has … _____

I have … _____

Who has … _____

I have … _____

Who has … _____

I have … _____

Who has … _____

I have … _____

FINISH

Social Studies Content
Example Lesson Featuring "Reconstruction"

Standards

- Acquire and use accurately a range of general academic and domain-specific words and phrases sufficient for reading, writing, speaking, and listening; demonstrate independence in gathering vocabulary knowledge when encountering an unknown term important to comprehension or expression.
- Determine central ideas or themes of a text and analyze their development; summarize the key supporting details and ideas.

Materials

- "Reconstruction" (page 83)
- *Social Studies Content for "Reconstruction"* (page 84)

Procedures

Introducing the Verse Text

- Allow students to read "Reconstruction" (page 83) silently.
- Then, read the poem aloud as students follow along. Be sure to model fluent, expressive reading. Have students read the poem chorally with partners and again as a class.
- Engage in a class discussion using the following questions as a guide:
  - ✳ Do you think the Southern leaders should have been punished or forgiven? Why?
  - ✳ What does "Reconstruction / was a bandage / on a wound / that ran far deeper" mean?
  - ✳ Why do slaves need to be taught how to be free?

Content-Based Strategy Steps

1. Before the lesson, cut apart the *Social Studies Content for "Reconstruction"* cards (page 84, socialstudies_reconstruction.pdf). Each card has the answer to a previous question and then asks a new question to keep the game going.
2. Distribute the cards to students. Depending on the number of students, you may choose to play with small groups, play multiple times, or have students team up with partners.
3. Begin the game by having the student with the "START" card read the question on the card. Then, the student with the answer to that question reads his or her card aloud. Students continue the game until they have reached the "FINISH" card. Offer clues from the verse text if students need assistance with the answers.
4. The cards should go in the order shown below.

> START; freedmen; segregation; 13th Amendment; Andrew Johnson; scalawag; 14th Amendment; sharecropping; Jim Crow Laws; Abraham Lincoln; 15th Amendment; carpetbagger

Reconstruction

By David L. Harrison

The once proud South
was on its knees.
Of every four men
who fought in battle,
one was dead.

So many wrecked lives . . .
so much poverty . . .
sad, burned out cities . . .
railroads, riverboats, bridges,
mostly gone.

How do you patch
a broken country?
Are Southern leaders
to be punished
or forgiven?

How do you help
four million slaves
cope, learn to be free?

For a dozen years
arguments raged
as Congress
and the president haggled.

Some say Reconstruction
was a bandage
on a wound
that ran far deeper.

Some say
it was a good start.

Some say
we have a long way to go.

WAR BETWEEN THE STATES

Name:_____ Date: _____

Social Studies Content for "Reconstruction"

START

Who has . . . the slaves who were freed?

I have . . . freedmen.

Who has . . . the separation of a race, class, or group of people?

I have . . . segregation.

Who has . . . the amendment that abolished slavery?

I have . . . the 13th Amendment.

Who has . . . the president after Abraham Lincoln was assassinated?

I have . . . Andrew Johnson.

Who has . . . a white Southerner who supported Reconstruction?

I have . . . scalawag.

Who has . . . the amendment that guarantees equal rights regardless of race?

I have . . . the 14th Amendment.

Who has . . . landowners leasing part of their land in return for a percentage of the crops?

I have . . . sharecropping.

Who has . . . the "separate but equal" laws that enforced segregation?

I have . . . Jim Crow Laws.

Who has . . . the president responsible for the Emancipation Proclamation?

I have . . . Abraham Lincoln.

Who has . . . the amendment that gives people the right to vote regardless of race?

I have . . . the 15th Amendment.

Who has . . . a white Northerner who came to help rebuild the South?

I have . . . carpetbagger.

FINISH

Poems About the 50 United States

Background Information on the Poems

Included on the digital resources online are two graphic maps (maps.pdf). These maps can be used alongside the poems about the 50 United States. You can display them for the class or distribute copies to students.

Poem	Background Information
Original Thirteen Colonies	The original thirteen colonies were made up of all kinds of people who wanted new lives. These people risked everything to board ships to the new colonies. Some of them died along the journey. In time, the colonies grew with many people who had made new lives for themselves. They took jobs as shipbuilders, merchants, and other craftsmen. Many of the colonists had different beliefs. They came to the New World seeking religious freedom. They learned to govern themselves under the eyes of Great Britain.
East	The Mississippi River is a long river that serves as the dividing line between the East Coast and the West Coast of the United States. The 26 states that lie east of the Mississippi River are referred to as the East Coast. These states have a variety of terrain such as mountains, swamps, beaches, and lakes. Some of these states are close to Canada while other states are close to the Great Lakes, the Atlantic Ocean, and the Gulf of Mexico.
Rhode Island	Rhode Island is the smallest state in the United States, but it has a large population of people and a coastline of 400 miles (643.7 km). Rhode Island is important to the history of the United States. This state was the first to get ready to fight against the British in the American Revolution. They wanted the Bill of Rights added to the Constitution. The Industrial Revolution in America started in Rhode Island with the creation of the water-powered cotton mill. Today, it continues to have industries that make a big impact on the country.
New York	New York plays an important role in the history of the United States. The state's history began with the American Indian tribes. They lived, hunted, and farmed on the land. Then, explorers came and took the land. The land was named after the Duke of York. In time, many people from other countries made the journey to New York to start new lives.

Background Information on the Poems *(cont.)*

Poem	Background Information
South	The South is a unique experience of food, hospitality, and traditions. Food like chitlins, catfish, and collard greens are common in southern restaurants and kitchens. Beautifully scented trees and flowering vines can be found there. Popular music of the South includes jazz and parade bands. The South is known for and is proud of its hospitality and friendliness. Southern states include Alabama, Kentucky, Mississippi, Tennessee, Arkansas, Louisiana, Oklahoma, Texas, Florida, Georgia, North Carolina, South Carolina, and Virginia.
Florida	From the beaches to the Kennedy Space Center to the horse races, Florida is known for its variety of attractions. Many people go fishing or boating in Florida because of the vast rivers, lakes, and ocean. Some people enjoy visiting the Florida Sports Hall of Fame. Others go to watch Florida's two major-league baseball teams. Many people enjoy eating key lime pie, a dessert made famous in Florida long ago. There is always something to do in Florida!
Louisiana	No place is more famous for its Creole and Cajun food than the state of Louisiana. People enjoy the special spices that make Louisiana gumbo and crawfish dishes so unique and flavorful. Rice and beans is another traditional dish for many families in Louisiana. Even after all the delicious meals, people still make room for a good dessert like sweet pecan pie.
Arkansas	The state of Arkansas got its name from the American Indian tribes who first lived there. The French explorers coined the name Arcansas. The land became part of the United States during the Louisiana Purchase and officially obtained statehood in 1826. This state is known for its beautiful underground caves, waterfalls, and national parks. Wildlife such as deer, elk, and bobcats roam its vast country land.
North Carolina	Queen Elizabeth sent John White to settle this colony. Some American Indian tribes did not get along with the colonists. Many ships have been lost along the rocky coast of this state. This state is home to Mount Mitchell, the highest peak of the Appalachian Mountains.

Background Information on the Poems *(cont.)*

Poem	Background Information
Georgia	The southern state of Georgia is known for its hospitality, good cooking, and beautiful scenery. Its people are very friendly. Georgia is known to grow some of the best peaches around. The state is home to a variety of wildlife and such beautiful trees as oak, hickory, and pine. It is also home to many beautiful mountains and beaches.
Illinois	The state of Illinois may be best known for being Abraham Lincoln's home state. He practiced law there and had a reputation for being an honest man. He served in the House of Representatives, too. He had strong feelings about slavery and about what was best for the country.
Ohio	There are many famous people from the state of Ohio. Ohio's nickname is the Buckeye State. This name originated from a small nut that grows in Ohio. This nut has a dark spot on it that makes it look like the eye of a buck, or a male deer.
Missouri	Missouri is known as the Show Me State. This phrase was made popular from a politician who once said, "I come from a state that raises corn and cotton and cockleburs and Democrats. . . . I am from Missouri. You have got to show me." The settlers who founded this state brought with them their cooking, their churches, and their schools. The state is home to the flowering dogwood. Missourians are a welcoming people and their surrounding scenery is beautiful.
Great Plains	The Great Plains are the states located in the middle of the United States. This includes Montana, South Dakota, North Dakota, Wyoming, Nebraska, Kansas, Colorado, Oklahoma, Texas, and New Mexico. All together, these states are larger than Alaska. While traveling through the Great Plains, you might see rivers, bison, and tall grasses. Long ago, the pioneers traveled through the Great Plains with their wagons, looking for a place to call home.
Texas	Many people know Texas as the place where cowboys and cattle roam. Long ago, the cowboy life was a hard life. They worked tiring, difficult days, and the trails were boring and lengthy. They often learned how to herd cattle while on the job.

Background Information on the Poems (cont.)

Poem	Background Information
Montana	Montana is known as Big Sky Country. It gets this name from the wide spaces that make the sky appear vast and endless. Montana is a beautiful place with stunning scenery that includes mountains, grasses, rivers, and plains. There are many animals including deer, mountain lions, and moose. People can ski, fish, hike, and visit the national parks, too. Montana gives the feeling of an open, large countryside that connects people back to nature.
California	Long ago, people who wanted to settle in California had to walk or travel in boats to get there. If they traveled in boats, they boarded the boat on the East Coast and traveled around South America. Some traveled to Panama, walked across the land, and boarded another ship to complete the journey. Today, California has a booming population. People can take buses, planes, trains, or automobiles to get to this great state.
Arizona	Arizona's history is rich with stories of the Wild West. One famous story involves a gunfight near the O.K. Corral in Tombstone. Though it only lasted about 30 seconds, many lives were lost in this famous gunfight. Wildlife of tarantulas, snakes, and scorpions live there. The amazing Grand Canyon is also located in Arizona. Visiting Arizona gives people the opportunity to see mountains, lakes, and miles of deserts.
Alaska	Alaska was sold to the United States for just two cents an acre. Not too long after, gold and oil were discovered there. Both of these discoveries enticed people to move there in hopes of striking it rich. Some people did get rich, but others went home penniless. Alaska is known for its rich, beautiful scenery and wildlife.
Hawaii	Long ago, people traveled from Polynesia to Hawaii. They paddled in canoes, found the islands, and began to populate them. European explorers came next. The Hawaiians did not want people from other countries controlling what they did. Hawaii had a leader, King Kamehameha, who united the islands to keep them independent. This special leader is celebrated today for his bravery and deeds.

Original Thirteen Colonies

By David L. Harrison

They came, the Dutch,
Swedes, Finns, English,
Quakers, Puritans,
Spanish, French, adventurers
by sea in crowded, pitching ships—
farmers, soldiers, men of trade,
seeking their way,
seeking freedom,
seeking new life in a new world.

Life was harsh,
many died;
many died
but others came,
seeking their way.

Others came and others came
until colonies grew
and many people
with different beliefs,
different customs,
different languages,
governed themselves in peace.

They were the ones
who risked all to become
The United States.

East

By David L. Harrison

We're the eastern states.
Know why?
That old Mississippi
lies somewhere to our west,
so we're East.

Twenty-six of us in all,
North, South, in between,
Maine, Wisconsin, Tennessee,
no matter whatever else we may be,
we're East.

Whether we neighbor Canada,
sit along the beach,
or ring around the Great Lakes,
we're East.

North, South, in between,
mountains, swamps, sand and sea,
no matter whatever else we may be,
that old Mississippi
lies somewhere to our west,
so we're East.

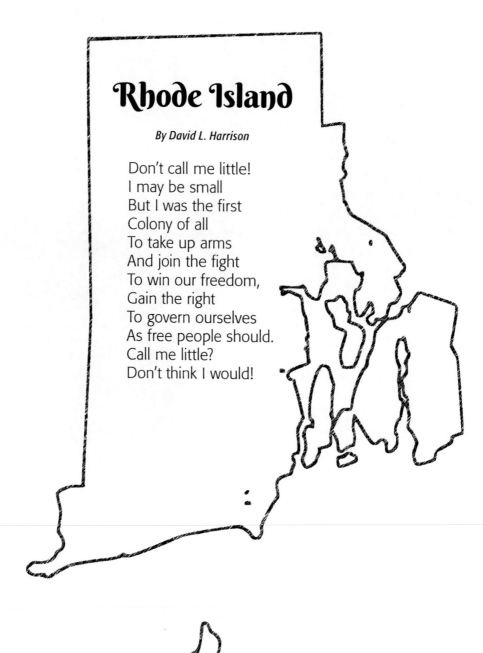

Rhode Island

By David L. Harrison

Don't call me little!
I may be small
But I was the first
Colony of all
To take up arms
And join the fight
To win our freedom,
Gain the right
To govern ourselves
As free people should.
Call me little?
Don't think I would!

New York

By David L. Harrison

We are a country of immigrants
and I am the state where many
first saw this great land.

One hundred million Americans
trace their roots
to weary travelers
just off boats and weeks at sea
who stood in lines as long as it took
to step at last on freedom's shore,
my shore.

I was named for an English duke,
but no one's more American than I.
I'm proud to be New York.

South

By David L. Harrison

I am the South and mighty proud of it.
Try my cooking, you're going to love it.
Chitlins, collard greens, honey baked hams,
Southern fried catfish, candied yams!
There's plenty more I want to say
About the South, the Southern way—
Jasmine flowers, humming bees,
Blossoms on magnolia trees,
Parades with local marching bands,
Jazz, banjos, Dixieland,
One thing I promise you will see—
My southern hospitality!

Florida

By David L. Harrison

Want to see some horses race?
I've got 'em.

See some rockets back from space?
I've got 'em.

Want to watch a baseball game?
See The Sports Hall of Fame?
I've got 'em.

Want to see some river otters?
I've got 'em.

Want to splash in sunny waters?
I've got 'em.

Want to try my Key Lime pie?
Fishing? Boating? Who can deny?
I've got 'em!

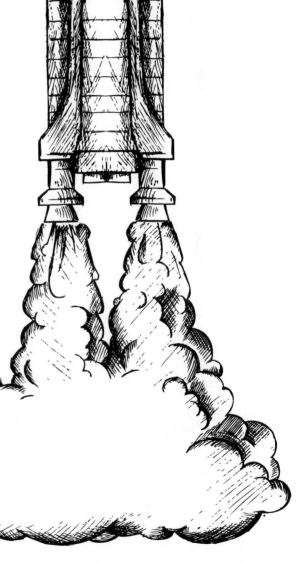

Louisiana

By David L. Harrison

Come on in,
I'll stir the pot!
Crawfish gumbo
Spicy hot.
Heap your plate
With rice and beans,
Jambalaya
From New Orleans.
Pat your tummy,
Heave a sigh,
Top it off
With pecan pie!

Arkansas

By David L. Harrison

Akakaze—
To the Quapaw it meant
"land of downriver people."
To the Dakota, it was
"people of the south wind."
The French pronounced it
Arcansas,
and so I was named.

My history runs deep
as limestone frosted caves
beneath my valleys,
clear as waterfalls plunging
into cold streams,
wild as bear, bobcat, elk,
nimble as a white-tailed deer.

I was proud to be America's
twenty-fifth state.
Come float my streams,
enjoy my beauty
in Arkansas.

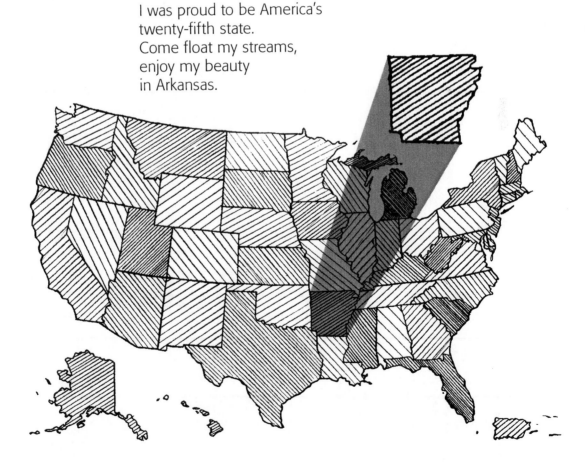

North Carolina

By David L. Harrison

From watery graves,
off Cape Hatteras
where lost ships sleep
to Mount Mitchell's craggy face
I offer you history tinted
through mists of time—
Indians who called this land their home,
Spanish conquistadors,
English settlers who risked all
to make this land theirs too.

I offer you river basins, rich soil
where melons, soybeans, cotton grow.

A modern state with ancient roots—
I offer you North Carolina.

Georgia

By David L. Harrison

I'm Georgia,
Land of grits and peaches,
Blue Ridge Mountains,
Sandy beaches,

Hospitality
Tried and true,
Good hearted people
Through and through.

Lots to see
in the deep south,
White-tailed deer,
Cottonmouth,
Woods of oak, pine, hickory,
Black coffee laced with chicory,

Magnolia blossoms,
Sweet iced tea,
Honeysuckle,
Honey bee.

No finer state will you ever find.
I've got Georgia on my mind.

Illinois

By David L. Harrison

I am The Land of Lincoln,
a reminder that our 16th president
lived, led, and died
at a crucial time in our history.

Young men marched off to fight,
to live or perish in someone's field
by musket ball or cannon fire.

Illinois sent over 250,000 into battle.
Nearly one man in every three
joined the war that in the end
purchased at an awful price
a more perfect union.

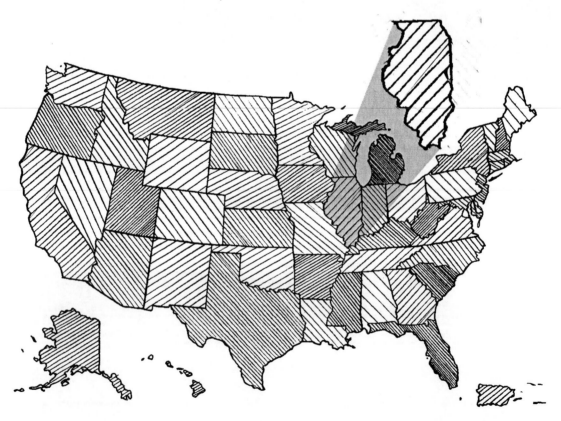

Ohio

By David L. Harrison

I'm O—*high in the middle*—O,
The Buckeye State, on the go.
I'm known for famous ladies, gents
Toni Morrison, presidents,
The Wright Brother's flight invention,
Edison's gifts, too many to mention.

John Glenn orbited Earth,
Neil Armstrong walked the moon,
Athletes, actors how their worth
The Mills Brothers used to croon;
I'm O—*high in the middle*—O,
The Buckeye State, on the go.

My shoreline's along Lake Erie,
Plan to come and see me, Dearie.
Catch a big league hockey game,
Visit Football Hall of Fame,
I'm O—*high in the middle*—O,
The Buckeye State, on the go!

Missouri

By David L. Harrison

Early Indians canoed my waters,
cupped their hands in clear springs,
drew bows in grass deer-high.

Explorers came,
settlers followed bringing Bibles,
fiddles, cooking pots,
building cabins, churches, schools,
bustling towns.

I'm Land of Dogwood,
bluebirds, bees,
farmers telling stories
with voices rich as fresh tilled soil.
Room for all, my mat is out,
Show Me State,
Missouri.

Great Plains

By David L. Harrison

North Dakota, South Dakota,
Kansas, Wyoming,
Where bison herds a million strong
Used to come roaming.

Texas, New Mexico,
Montana, Nebraska,
Colorado, Oklahoma—
We're bigger than Alaska!

Back when pioneers came west,
Their wagons rolled this way
Leaving tracks dug down so deep
You still see some today.

Through tall prairie grass they came,
Across wide rivers too,
They risked everything they had
To start their lives anew.

Texas

By David L. Harrison

One hundred fifty years ago,
If you were alive,
You might have been a cowboy
On a cattle drive
From west Texas all the way
To Abilene
With more cows than anyone
Had ever seen.
Forty thousand cowboys worked
The trails back then.
You can call them cowboys, son,
I call them men.

Montana

By David L. Harrison

Soaring eagle,
Grizzly bear,
Cedar scented
Forest air,
Belly River,
Flathead Lake,
Winters so cold
Your bones ache,
Jagged peaks,
Mountain passes,
Great plains,
Prairie grasses,
Big Hole Valley,
Lodgepole pine,
Cutthroat trout
Fighting your line,
Big sky,
Quiet places,
Montana folks
Like open spaces.

California

By David L. Harrison

Why would anyone walk to California?
Well long ago it was all that you could do,
There were no planes or trains or cars or buses,
So unless you went by boat you went by shoe.

Just think how hard it was to make the journey,
But more than 40,000 people hiked it,
Took six months to cross those lonely miles,
I bet you no one's feet ever liked it.

Today I'm home to thirty-seven million,
The most any state has had before,
They come from every nation on the planet,
And no one has to walk here anymore!

Arizona

By David L. Harrison

I became a state in 1912,
nearly 400 years after Coronado
came looking for cities of gold;
what he found was
poor Indians' pueblos.

I was wild and woolly in my day!
Navajo attacks on Fort Defiance,
bitter battles during the Civil War,
gunfight at the O.K. Corral,
some pretty scary characters in Tombstone.

Had a lot of longhorn cows—
more than a million of 'em—
copper mining and railroads
made some folks mighty rich.

I've got it all,
mountain lakes to deserts,
bustling cities to the Grand Canyon.
Never mind the snakes and scorpions,
tarantulas aren't going to bother you.
Come on out!
The weather's a little warm at times,
but it's a nice, dry sort of heat.

Alaska

By David L. Harrison

I may not look it
but I started out poor!
In 1867 I was worth
two measly cents an acre.

But thirty years later
guess what happened?
Gold!
Gold! Gold! Gold! Gold!
Thousands of folks
came tearing up here
to strike it rich! Well . . .

Some did,
most went home broke.

Then it happened again:
Oil!
Billions of barrels that flow
through my pipes
like a vein stretching 800 miles.

But I'm not all about making money.
Come taste my berries,
watch my elk herds,
hike on my glaciers,
look up at my mountains and yell,
"Wow!"

Don't like to brag, but I'm mighty pretty,
so pack a bag,
bring a camera,
plan to stay a while.

Hawaii

By David L. Harrison

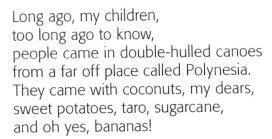

Long ago, my children,
too long ago to know,
people came in double-hulled canoes
from a far off place called Polynesia.
They came with coconuts, my dears,
sweet potatoes, taro, sugarcane,
and oh yes, bananas!

From then 'til now much has occurred:
English named us Sandwich Islands,
Russians came, built forts,
French talked much of freedom
of religion.

We survived it all, my children,
a proud people with proud heritage,
eight big islands of us,
more than one hundred others,
brought together by King Kamehameha.
If you can pronounce that, my dears,
I'll call you my little Hawaiians.

Poems About American History

Background Information on the Poems

Poem	Background Information
First People	Traditional history teaches that the first people in North America came from eastern Asia to Alaska by crossing a land bridge called Beringia (now the Bering Strait) about 13,500 years ago. These groups of people migrated throughout the continent. However, in the past decade, this theory has been debated as more archaeological evidence comes to light.
American Indians	Before the arrival of European settlers, the continental United States was home to eight cultural areas of American Indians. Tribes in the Northeast, Southeast, and Southwest built permanent settlements and farmed. Others, like the Plains and Great Basin tribes, were nomadic. Tribes in California, the Northwest, and the Plateau were hunter/gatherers, and they used the ocean and streams to provide for their needs.
Explorer	Many people explored the new land called America, but Christopher Columbus is the most famous. When he stumbled upon the continent in 1492, he thought he had found a shortcut to the West Indies. Other explorers include Amerigo Vespucci, who realized Columbus had not found Asia but a new continent. Juan Ponce de Leon is also famous for his exploration of Florida.
Jamestown, 1615	Founded in 1607, Jamestown was the first permanent English settlement in the New World. A little over 100 men arrived, but many were from wealthy families and did not know how to farm. The Powhatan tribe lived nearby. At first, the settlers and the Powhatan got along. The Powhatan people would send food to the settlers. Over time, the relationship worsened as the settlers demanded too much food. The winter of 1609–1610 was called "The Starving Time" because 80 percent of the colonists died of starvation.
Pilgrims	In 1620, over 100 people sailed to what is now Cape Cod, Massachusetts, for religious freedom. They named the new settlement Plymouth Colony. They arrived in late fall, and the winter was very harsh. Over half of the group died because of inadequate shelter. In the spring of 1621, they met Squanto, an English-speaking American Indian. He and the Pokanoket Wampanoag tribe helped the Pilgrims. They shared the now-famous Thanksgiving feast in 1621.

Background Information on the Poems (cont.)

Poem	Background Information
Puritan Woman	In the late sixteenth century, England sought to reform the Church of Rome into the Church of England. Many felt the Church of England was not reformed enough and wanted to purify their religion further. These "Puritans" began experiencing religious persecution. By 1641, over 21,000 Puritans had left Europe and moved to America. This group was characterized by their devotion to God. They believed that husbands were the spiritual leaders of the households, and that wives should be obedient to their husbands. They believed that women should only be in charge of the home.
American Colonies	The original thirteen colonies included Massachusetts, Connecticut, Rhode Island, New York, New Jersey, New Hampshire, Pennsylvania, Delaware, Maryland, Virginia, North Carolina, South Carolina, and Georgia. In 1700, there were about 250,000 people in the colonies. Though times were hard, the colonists flourished to over 2.5 million people by the time the Revolutionary War started in 1776.
Militiaman	The militiamen were ordinary citizens who served in the Revolutionary War despite having no formal military training. Disorganized and without uniforms, standard weapons, or supplies, they were the clear underdogs in the war for freedom.
General George Washington	George Washington was a successful and wealthy farmer in Virginia. Before the Revolutionary War, he served during the French and Indian War. When the Revolutionary War started, he was a natural choice for leadership because of his bravery and intelligence.
Constitution	The Articles of Confederation were written to serve as America's laws during the Revolutionary War. After the war, however, the founding fathers realized that a new document was needed. The Constitution was the answer, written during the summer of 1787 in Philadelphia. The United States began operating under the new law of the land on March 9, 1789.

Background Information on the Poems *(cont.)*

Poem	Background Information
Why the President Is the President	As George Washington was the first elected president, the citizens of the newly formed United States were not sure how to address him. The debate over title became very intense, but eventually "Mr. President" was accepted (and "Madam President" for a woman).
Lewis and Clark	Meriwether Lewis, William Clark, and a small group of men set out in May 1804 from St. Louis, Missouri to map the newly acquired Louisiana Purchase. The American Indian Sacagawea joined them as a guide. For over two years, they explored the rugged Midwest looking for water passage to the Pacific Ocean, establishing American presence, and discovering new plant and animal life.
What Does He Want?	Relationships between the American Indians and early colonists were complicated at best. At times, a fragile truce allowed for helpful trading—American Indians traded furs, food, and farming knowledge to the colonists for weapons, cooking utensils, and fishing hooks. But much more common were broken treaties, the spreading of diseases, and fighting over land.
War of 1812	Sometimes called "America's Second War for Independence," the War of 1812 was fought between the young United States and Great Britain. Canada and American Indians were also involved. After Fort McHenry in Baltimore withstood a 25-hour attack from the English Navy, Francis Scott Key famously wrote "The Star-Spangled Banner," which later became the National Anthem. The War of 1812 left Americans with a sense of pride and patriotism.
Pioneers	By 1840, over seven million Americans had traveled the long and dangerous route to the western territories. Hoping to make new lives for themselves by owning and farming their own land, families headed west with their wagons and only the bare essentials. The phrase *Manifest Destiny* is often used with westward expansion. It describes not only the spirit of determination and independence the pioneers had but also their belief that God had destined the land to belong to the United States.

Background Information on the Poems (cont.)

Poem	Background Information
Slave	While slaves could not legally marry, some slaves still married one another informally. Slave families lived in constant fear of being separated. Some men and women had an "abroad marriage," where the husband lived on a neighboring farm and came to visit his family twice a week. Young slaves began to work as early as seven or eight years old. Males were desired because of their ability to do outdoor labor. Boys were in more danger of the slave owners separating them from their families.
Civil War by a Wounded Soldier	The Civil War not only divided the country but also many families. States such as Delaware, Missouri, Kentucky, Maryland, and West Virginia were on the border of Union and Confederate states. Members within the same family often had—and fought for—differing opinions on slavery. Even Abraham Lincoln's family was divided, as most of his in-laws sided with the Confederacy.
Civil War	From the Civil War's beginning in 1861 until its end in 1865, over 620,000 American soldiers died. More recent accounts claim the number may be closer to 750,000. Many soldiers died on the battlefield, but two-thirds of the deaths were caused by disease. The idea of germs was not yet understood, and antiseptics were not available. The soldiers who did return home often did so with lifelong injuries.
Reconstruction	After the Civil War, much of the South was in ruins. The Reconstruction period lasted from 1865–1877. There were two goals during Reconstruction: to help rebuild the South and to reform the Union. Congress also passed three amendments to the Constitution: the 13th, which outlawed slavery; the 14th, which made African Americans citizens; and the 15th, which gave male African Americans the right to vote.
Ellis Island	Ellis Island is a small island in New York Harbor that neighbors the Statue of Liberty. At one time, it was the busiest federal immigration center. While open from 1892–1954, more than 12 million immigrants passed through the center. Over 80 percent were accepted to enter within the normal three- to seven-hour range, but others were detained for days or weeks at a time because of illness. The first immigrant to pass through was Annie Moore from Ireland on January 1, 1892.

First People

By David L. Harrison

There was a time long ago,
Before Dakota, Arapaho,
Cheyenne, Apache, Navajo,

When not a single human stirred
And neither wild beast nor bird
Had ever heard a human word,

But one day came the first man,
First woman, first clan,
And human history here began,

Before Comanche, Pawnee, Crow,
Cherokee, Blackfoot, Arapaho,
Shoshone, Shawnee, Navajo.

American Indians

By David L. Harrison

Our tribes were many, our nations strong.
From the Great Plains to the bountiful sea
We danced our dance, sang our song.

Mostly our people got along,
Lived their lives in harmony,
Our tribes were many, our nations strong.

Our customs were old, our memory long.
Throughout our ancient history
We danced our dance, sang our song.

We taught our children to belong,
To learn their part so they could see
Our tribes were many, our nations strong.

To kill more than we needed was wrong.
As our animal brothers roamed free,
We danced our dance, sang our song.

We didn't know of the coming throng
Of men who wouldn't let us be.
Our tribes were many, our nations strong.
We danced our dance, sang our song.

Explorer

By David L. Harrison

I am the brave explorer,
I sail across the sea
To claim your land
For king or queen,
You are no longer free.

I am the brave explorer,
Determined, valiant, bold,
I load my ships
With what I want,
I seek your cities of gold.

I am the brave explorer,
Your treasures go with me,
I'll be rewarded
When I sail
Back home across the sea.

Jamestown, 1615

By David L. Harrison

My name is Bartholomew Hoskins,
fifteen years of age.
Late of London, I arrived last week
to seek my way in this New World.

I praise God I was spared
being present in the beginning.
For those bone-weary travelers,
no rosy hearth awaited,
no bounty ripening in the field,
no streets to stroll
and tip one's hat to neighbors.

Bitter winter awaited,
Indian attacks, dysentery,
frozen muddy trails
between hovels
cramped and hastily constructed.
Starvation awaited.

With too many gentlemen
and too few men to work,
those poor souls were doomed.
They chose a swampy site
with brackish water unfit to drink,
mosquitoes in relentless swarms of torment,
arrows, those devil darts,
that left their victims
writhing on a wooded path,
painting the leaves crimson.

I read this in the public log
of that first awful August, 1607.

> The sixth day, there died John Asbie, of
> the bloody flux.
> The ninth day, died William Bruster,
> Gentleman,
> of a wound given by the Savages.
> The tenth day, died George Flowre, of the
> swelling.
> The fourteenth day, Jerome Alikock, of a
> wound;
> the same day, Francis Midwinter and
> Edward Moris died suddenly.

One hundred two men landed.
Nearly half were dead by spring.

Five hundred more came.
Of every eight, seven died
during the starving winter of 1609.

Walking skeletons stalked the fields,
scavenging for the slightest scrap,
while Indians were killing as fast without
as famine and pestilence were within.

The colony has moved upriver
and conditions are improved,
but I must tell you I worry.
What will happen to me
in this place of misery and dying dreams?

In this colony—this Jamestown—
will it be written that Bartholomew Hoskins,
late of London,
perished here on New World soil,
or prospered?

Pilgrims

By David L. Harrison

We sought freedom
from religious persecution,
freedom to worship God
as we saw fit.

One hundred two of us
sold our possessions,
packed our Geneva Bibles,
left Europe and our homes behind,
and boarded the Mayflower
to cross the Atlantic's stormy seas.

In spite of our misery
and the loss of two lives,
we wrote a sacred covenant
to govern ourselves
in the New World.
All our members
would be treated as equals.

After ten long weeks we landed,
cold and miserable,
death our close companion.
Only fifty-three survived to spring.

We were humble folk
accustomed to toil,
seeking only freedom.
We made our way never dreaming
that our sacred covenant
laid down the beginnings
for a great future democracy.
One day we would be part of history.
One day we would be known as
the Pilgrims.

Puritan Woman

By David L. Harrison

I am a Puritan woman.
My job is to obey my husband,
bear his children, raise them to be
obedient, God-fearing boys and girls.

Is life hard?
Oftentimes it seems so.
Last week I buried my oldest.
Sat some time in silence,
but there was much to do
besides mourning.

My job is to spin yarn from wool,
knit our sweaters and stockings,
make soap, dip candles,
churn cream into butter,
prepare food for the table.

I'm not allowed to own so much
as the clothes upon my back.
I cannot vote on colony affairs.
My husband attends
to such weighty matters.

Is life hard?
Oftentimes it seems so.
I am a Puritan woman.

American Colonies

By David L. Harrison

We came as English, Finns, Swedes,
French, Poles, Portuguese,
Germans, Dutch, Spanish, Irish,
Bringing our ways across the seas.

We came with our own allegiances,
Established colonies as they were planned.
Up and down the New World
We built our churches, tilled the land.

Though many settlers met ill fate,
Through the years our colonies grew
Until we stood up to Parliament
For dictating what they required us to do.

We made our decision: revolution!
Brave men left village and farms.
The British scoffed and thought they'd whip us
When our raggedy militia took up arms.

But now we came as one people,
One future, not thirteen fates.
We came now as a fledgling nation
The world would know as United States.

Militiaman

By David L. Harrison

Never been so cold,
not in the worst of times,
nor so hungry.

Those Redcoats in their fancy uniforms,
marching in rank in their warm boots,
bellies full, I imagine; their fancy guns
cleaned and oiled and ready to kill us.

What if I die in this barren field?
Never see my mother again,
father, baby brother …
Never been so scared.

But this morning!
General George Washington himself
rode right into camp!
Striding that great horse,
he looked me steady in the eye.
Me!

"Son," he said, "those British lads
are an ocean away from home.
They're not fighting for their own land,
they're fighting for yours.
You live here.
This is your home.
We shall not let them take your home."

General George Washington himself said that!
He told me we're going to win.
He told me one of these days
we're going to win,
and we'll all go home.

Never been so cold.
And I'm plenty scared!
But I believe General George Washington.
He told me we're going to win,
and I believe him.

General George Washington

By David L. Harrison

I saw a lad this morning,
no different, really,
from thousands of others,
shivering over a meager fire,
attempting to warm his feet
where they stuck through
holes in his boots.

Pale, gaunt as a starving wolf,
he looked tempted
to boil his boots for supper,
nor would he be the first.

Wherever I go it's the same,
exhausted men perishing in the cold,
wasting away from hunger.
Yet there are those in Congress
who do not see
the plight of these men,
their desperate need for warm clothes,
boots, food . . .

We would lose this war
but for these brave fighters.
They look to me to lead them to victory.
I can do no less.
I tell them, in spite of all odds,
we shall prevail.

I must, and I do believe,
that we shall persevere.
But victory comes at a terrible price.
It cannot come too soon!

Constitution

By David L. Harrison

"We the people of the United States,"
is how it begins,
"in order to form a more perfect union . . ."

Brilliant men came together
for a common cause—
to write a constitution
for our new nation,
write it to establish justice,
spell out the rules
that would govern and protect its citizens
for all time to come.

Washington, Jefferson, Hamilton, Madison . . .
they and 51 others
debated, haggled, shouted, compromised for 116 days.
In spite of all differences,
against all odds,
they created a shining document,
a torch of freedom held high for all who would follow:
a constitution,
their constitution,
our Constitution of the United States of America.

Why the President Is the President

By David L. Harrison

When General George Washington
became our first president
in 1789, an important question was,
"What should people call him?"

The House of Representatives said,
"He is president to all the people.
He needs no title, call him
George Washington.
Call him
President of the United States."

But the Senate said,
"*President* sounds too
common.
Cricket clubs have presidents.
Fire companies have presidents.
We should call him
Excellency."

Said some, "Call him,
His Highness the President
of the United States of America
and Protector of the Rights of Same."

Faces flushed red.
Angry shouts filled the chamber.
This was serious business!
This was a statement
about who we were,
who we wanted to be.

The debate lasted long and hot.
After a month the vote was taken,
and so it was that

George Washington
and all the presidents to follow
would henceforth be called—
simply, with dignity, with respect—
The President of the United States.

Lewis and Clark

By David L. Harrison

The Louisiana Purchase
took in a lot of land.
President Jefferson wondered
just what we'd bought
so in 1804 he sent us
on an expedition to find out.

Could we travel by water
to the great Pacific,
he wanted to know.
How many Indian nations dwelled
by mighty rivers?
Hunted on endless plains?
Who were they?
What could be taught
and learned?

Well let me tell you
it was a mercy we survived!
And without a certain Shoshone
named Sacagawea,
we never would have made it,
that's a fact!

Our perilous journey
took us up the Missouri,
across the Continental Divide,
down the Clearwater,
the Snake, the Columbia,
past Portland
at last to the sea.

From the time we met Sacagawea
in South Dakota territory,
she found plants we could eat,
talked to other Indian tribes,

bartered for our horses—
all while carrying her own baby!

We learned a lot.
Indians? Plenty. 72 tribes!
Mostly friendly.
Without their help
we would have perished
from cold and gnawing hunger
during two bitter winters.

Plants and animals?
Found 200 new ones!
Maps? Made 140.

Well we made it,
and I'll tell you something
I believe is true.
History will long remember
the Lewis and Clark Expedition!

29 USA

SACAGAWEA

What Does He Want?

(2 voices)

By David L. Harrison

Indian	*White Man*
The white man comes.	
What does he want?	The Indian is here. What does he want?
	Calls himself the first people.
Does he want to own the land?	
	What will he do? Fight? Surrender?
Does he want to own *us*?	
	Sign our treaties.
The white man comes.	
	The Indian is here.
Some are friendly, Some are not.	Some are friendly, Some are not.
What does he want?	What does he want?
Should I trust him? Can I trust him?	Should I trust him? Can I trust him?
What does he want? Why is he here?	What does he want?

War of 1812

By David L. Harrison

From New Orleans to Canada
The war was fought on land and sea
To settle once and forevermore
The right of America to be free.

It could have ended either way.
Raging on at terrible cost
The tides of fortune ebbed and flowed
With bitter battles won and lost.

The British burned our capitol,
The White House blazed the night red,
The color of blood shed by all
Those sacrificing honored dead.

Our national anthem sprang from the heart
And mind of Francis Scott Key.
By rockets' glare throughout the night
He penned, "Oh say can you see!"

Today as proud Americans
With hands to hearts we gladly sing,
Grateful for our brave forefathers,
For one and all, "Let freedom ring!"

Pioneers

By David L. Harrison

No interstates,
no highways,
no roads, paved or graveled.
Only trails toward the westward sun,
scarred and rutted by iron clad wheels
of wagons creaking under loads
of what families needed along the way
and at the end of their journey.

No room for passengers
except the weak and ill
amid the stores of food,
dishes, clothing, furniture,
tools, bedding . . .

Lucky ones rode horses or mules,
others walked by their wagons,
struggling ten miles a day,
month after weary month
for half a year through heat,
flooded rivers, hostile territory.

Yet they came,
and still they came,
determined folks determined
to start anew in a new world.
They peopled the west,
ensured the future
of young America.

Slave

By David L. Harrison

I'm scared.
Even when he hits me
I can't stop crying.
"Shut up," old master says.
"Stand up straight."

Old master he sell me.
Mama? Daddy?
I got no family!
Can't stop crying.

"Pull those weeds!"
new master says.
I don't know where I am.
Mama? Daddy?

He hits me for crying,
kicks me for missing a weed.
I stop crying—
on the outside.

Civil War by a Wounded Soldier

By David L. Harrison

Reckon this wound
is going to kill me.
I don't care.
Pa told me, "Don't come home."
He said, "No Yankee is a son of mine."
Got a musket ball in my thigh.
Reckon I don't care if I die.
However this bitter fight turns out,
I'm already dead at home.

Civil War

By David L. Harrison

And it came to this:
our young nation so divided
that war—
most unspeakable horror—
was the only answer.

By thunder of cannon
and musket rattle,
by screams of dying young men,
would the fate of our future be met.

One soldier died in every five,
often buried where they fell.
Four bloody years of carnage,
six hundred twenty thousand dead,
homes burned, families ripped apart.

Slavery was a cancer,
war, the terrible surgery
that destroyed in order to build
a more perfect union.

Reconstruction

By David L. Harrison

The once proud South
was on its knees.
Of every four men
who fought in battle,
one was dead.

So many wrecked lives . . .
so much poverty . . .
sad, burned out cities . . .
railroads, riverboats, bridges,
mostly gone.

How do you patch
a broken country?
Are Southern leaders
to be punished
or forgiven?

How do you help
four million slaves
cope, learn to be free?

For a dozen years
arguments raged
as Congress
and the president haggled.

Some say Reconstruction
was a bandage
on a wound
that ran far deeper.

Some say
it was a good start.

Some say
we have a long way to go.

WAR BETWEEN THE STATES

Ellis Island

By David L. Harrison

By the hundreds they come,
dragging, toting possessions
like peddlers to market
in pockets, baskets,
cardboard boxes,
leather sacks,
on their heads and backs,
the most precious, in their hearts.

The Frelingers from France,
who will settle in Kentucky
to be iron dealers and blacksmiths.

The Andersons from Norway,
to be ship fitters out of New York.

In endless snaking lines
they start-stop-start along,
hugging their children close
amid the nervous babble of languages
echoing around the vaulted hall.

Canio DeLoca from Italy,
ice-cream maker.

Conrad Rasinski from Poland,
musician who will perform
in John Phillip Sousa's band.

By the hundreds,
        the thousands they come.
America!
So close they can see it,
almost smell it,
feel its pulse beckoning
them!

The Oelrichs from Germany,
fun loving musical farmers
who will settle in Iowa
for 40 acres and a mule.

Joe and Maria Giuseppe from Italy,
will settle in Ohio
where Joe will work a production line
for B.F. Goodrich.

Stanislaus Dombek from Poland,
who will mine for coal in Pennsylvania.

A few more questions,
forms, examinations . . .

The Yolens from Ukraine,
bottlers with money in their pockets
who will settle near New Haven,
produce tradesmen,
journalists, artisans.

By the hundreds,
        the thousands,
                the millions they come
through the great gate
that opens on their dreams,
their new life,
their America.

Poems About Ancient Civilizations

Background Information on the Poems

The Poems About Ancient Civilizations use abbreviations referring to the Common Era. "Before the Common Era" is abbreviated as B.C.E. "Common Era" is abbreviated as C.E.

Poem	Background Information
After the Hunt— Middle Paleolithic (140,000–40,000 B.C.E.)	Evidence shows the Middle Paleolithic man participated in behavior such as burying the dead, trading, and using fire to cook or smoke food. Beads, painted rocks, and marked elephant tusks point to artistic expression as well.
Before the Pharaohs—Middle Pleistocene (120,000 B.C.E.)	The Middle Pleistocene time period coincides partially with the Middle Paleolithic era. The former is a more geological classification referring to the Pleistocene "Ice Age." The latter is a more sociological term that marks the beginning of humans using stone tools.
The Farmer— Neolithic (10,000–2000 B.C.E.)	The Neolithic time period is the later part of the Stone Age. Man began creating permanent or seasonal settlements and farmed wild and domesticated crops. They even had some domesticated animals such as goats, sheep, and dogs.
Mehrgarh— Ancient India (7000 B.C.E.)	The ruins of Mehrgarh were found in 1974 and showed one of the earliest examples of a permanent herding and farming settlement. The people lived in mud-brick houses and grew barley, wheat, dates, and jujubes. They also made beads and did metal work.
Pharaoh— Ancient Egypt (3100–30 B.C.E.)	Pharaoh was the political and religious leader of ancient Egypt. He was considered a god on Earth; as such, he owned all the land in Egypt, made laws, taxed the people, and was expected to protect the country. Pharaohs famously built huge pyramids filled with treasure and servants to take with them to the afterlife.

Background Information on the Poems *(cont.)*

Poem	Background Information
Common Folk– Ancient Egypt (3100–30 B.C.E.)	While ancient Egypt is famous for the lavish and extravagant wealth of the pharaoh, less is known about the plight of the commoners. Archaeological evidence suggests many Egyptians were poor farmers or laborers. An ancient cemetery of lower-class Egyptians shows that many were malnourished with broken bones and joint diseases.
Cradle of Civilization– Mesopotamia (3100–539 B.C.E.)	From the Greek for "two rivers," Mesopotamia is credited with important developments including the idea of a developing city, written language, and the invention of the wheel. Women in Mesopotamia enjoyed equal rights with men and could own land, get divorced, and have their own businesses.
Sacred Cows– India (apx. 3000 B.C.E.)	Cows are honored and revered in India, but they are not worshipped as many believe. Cows are seen as a symbol of life, so Hindus stopped eating beef thousands of years ago for both practical and spiritual reasons. Though cows are not treated any differently from other animals on most days, they are honored on Gopastami, the cow holiday.
Gifts of the Mayans (2600 B.C.E.)	Located in what is now Guatemala and parts of Mexico, the Mayan empire had many cities with a total population near two million people. They were deeply religious, worshipped many gods, and built elaborate temples. They also had an extensive written language, advanced mathematics, and an accurate calendar. The Mayans reached their peak population around 250 C.E., and by 900 C.E., the empire was abandoned for unknown reasons.
Rise and Fall– Babylon (2300–539 B.C.E.)	Babylon is the most famous city in Mesopotamia, which is now Iraq. The city's modern-day fame is due in part to its unfavorable mentioning in the Bible. As a center for learning, culture, art, and gardens, it was one of the first cultures to have written laws.

Background Information on the Poems (cont.)

Poem	Background Information
If This Temple Could Talk– Mayans (2000 B.C.E.)	During the Mayan empire, two types of pyramids were built. Both were built for the gods, but one had a temple on top so the priest could climb to the highest point to offer sacrifices. The other pyramid was a sacred gift to the gods and was too steep to climb. Today, some of the pyramids and temples have been restored and are accessible for tourists to visit. Others are covered in wild, overgrown jungles.
Biblical–Israelites (1500 B.C.E.)	According to the Bible, God promised Abraham he would be a father of many nations. His grandson, Jacob (who was later known as Israel), had 12 sons who founded the 12 tribes of Israel. The Israelites are said to be God's chosen people, and they experienced periods of both blessing and discipline.
Archaeology– Israelites (1500 B.C.E.)	The Bible chronicles the story of the Israelites from their beginnings as sons of Jacob to their enslavement in Egypt to their eventual pilgrimage ending in the promised land. Archaeologists from both biblical and secular mindsets continue to learn more about the tribe's past.
Oracle Bones from the Shang Dynasty– Ancient China (1200 B.C.E.)	Oracle bones were used by the ancient Chinese to tell the future. Priests would write questions to the ancestors using oxen shoulder bones or turtle shells. When heated, the bones would crack and priests would "read" the cracks to find answers about future events.
The Olympics Begin– Greece (776 B.C.E.)	The ancient Olympics were held every four years from around 776 B.C.E. until 393 C.E. Running races were the only events for the first several games, but slowly, other events were introduced. A one-month truce was called across Greece during the Olympics because there was usually war going on, and thousands of people came to Olympia to watch. The modern games were introduced in 1896.

Background Information on the Poems (cont.)

Poem	Background Information
Athens—Greece (479–323 B.C.E.)	Athens is named for Athena, the Greek goddess of war and wisdom. It is one of the oldest cities in the world. It has been a continuous home for people for over 3000 years. There was no king in Athens; the Greeks invented democracy. They also built elaborate temples such as the Parthenon, which still stands today.
School—Rome (300 B.C.E.)	During the Roman Republic, children were often taught at home. This informal education included basic reading and writing. As the republic grew into the Roman Empire, the Romans began modeling their education after the Greeks. Tuition-based schools were started, and Greek teachers and tutors were often employed.
Terra-cotta Army—China (250 B.C.E.)	China's first emperor, Qin Shi Huang Di, commissioned the creation of what is now known as the "Terra-cotta Army." The army consists of thousands of soldiers and horses made from clay. The bodies seem to be made in an assembly-line fashion, but the faces are unique. Many of the soldiers hold real weapons, and it is thought the emperor wanted their protection in the afterlife.
Julius Caesar—Rome (46–44 B.C.E.)	Born in July 100 B.C.E. in the Roman Republic, Julius Caesar grew up to be considered one of the greatest military minds of all time. Under his reign, Rome grew to be a mighty empire. He declared himself the dictator of the Roman Empire for life and began making many positive changes. He also made many enemies and was assassinated in 44 B.C.E.
The Colosseum—Rome (80 C.E.)	The Colosseum was built in less than 10 years and opened to the public in 80 C.E. with 100 days of games. Admission was free, and the Colosseum could seat 50,000 people. The structure was used for over 400 years for such events as gladiator fights, wild-animal displays, religious ceremonies, and executions. It is estimated that over half a million people and one million animals lost their lives in the Colosseum.

After the Hunt—Middle Paleolithic (140,000–40,000 B.C.E.)

By David L. Harrison

Ahhh . . .
      too full to move . . .
        sore! . . .
          sleepy . . .
fire feels warm . . .

The beast fought hard,
trampled many spears,
screaming,
thrashing its trunk.

We screamed louder
as our stone points flew,
struck, cut deep,
again and again.

We will feast for many days.

Tomorrow we make more spears,
chip more points sharp enough
to pierce thick hides . . .
smoke all the meat
the women can carry . . .
      tomorrow . . .

Tonight . . .
    ahhh . . .
        fire is warm . . .
          eyes grow . . .
heavy . . .
   I sleep.

Before the Pharaohs—
Middle Pleistocene
(120,000 B.C.E.)

By David L. Harrison

The soil beside the river
was rich and fertile.
Plants prospered in abundance,
animals grazed or hunted,
according to their kind.
The valley was bountiful
when the first people came.

They hunted with stone weapons,
ate plants along the banks,
dined on carcasses
left by predators.
Life was slow to change.

One day this place
would be called Egypt,
this river the Nile.
But not for 100,000 years.

For now these egg snatchers,
fruit pickers, nut crackers, fish catchers,
these hunters and gatherers,
would live in the valley
and call it home.

Egypt and its pharaohs,
its mighty kings and wars,
were not yet part
of anyone's dream.

The Farmer—Neolithic (10,000–2000 B.C.E.)

By David L. Harrison

There came a time 12,000 years ago
when people started settling down, keeping
dogs, raising sheep and goats, planting
wheat, gathering wild crops, banding

Together in settled camps instead of following
migrating herds, hunting meat with spears
and sharp points fashioned from brittle stone.

Farming gave them time to make pots,
weave baskets from reeds, bark, leather,
improve clothing, invent tools, art.

There came a time 12,000 years ago
when planting and harvesting small grains of wheat
forever changed the lives of all who followed.

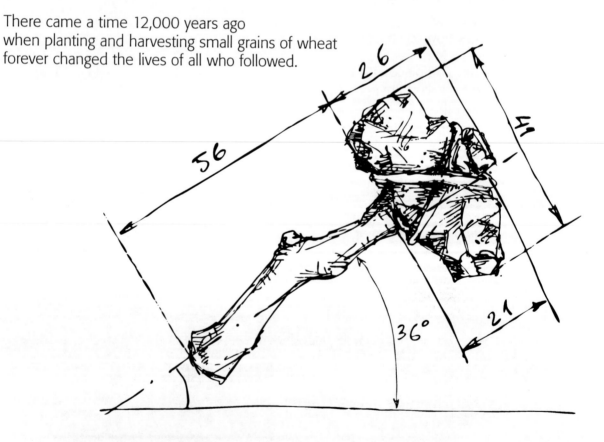

Mehrgarh—Ancient India (7000 B.C.E.)

By David L. Harrison

Where early wanderers settled down
To build the oldest known town
And farmers cultivated land,
Ancient Indian history began,
At Mehrgarh.

They irrigated, planted wheat,
Hunted less and raised their meat,
Modeled figures out of clay,
Sophisticated for their day,
In Mehrgarh.

They satisfied their jewelry needs
With bangles, ornaments, and beads,
Worked as no one had before
To fashion tools from copper ore,
Traded far off tribes for goods
Worked with leather, stones, woods,
In Mehrgarh.

Where once the streets were filled with noise
From barking dogs and yelling boys,
Neighbors calling out their greetings,
Tribal leaders off to meetings,
Now the silence is profound
In the oldest city ever found,
In Mehrgarh.

Pharaoh—Ancient Egypt (3100–30 B.C.E.)

By David L. Harrison

I am Pharaoh.
Almighty ruler.
King. Monarch.
God on Earth!

I, Pharaoh,
own the land.

I declare wars.
I build temples.

And this, too, I do—
I build monuments
to glorify myself.
Let all men know
of my wondrous deeds!

Let thousands toil
day and night
for twenty years
to built a pyramid
glorious enough
to escort me
to the afterlife.

Let my servants be honored.
Upon my death,
kill them and bury them with me.
I will need their services
when I ascend
to join the other gods.
I am Pharaoh.

Common Folk—Ancient Egypt
(3100–30 B.C.E.)

By David L. Harrison

In ancient Egypt every person
knew his job and status.
Under pharaoh
came his vizier,
then administrators.
Next came physicians, engineers,
priests, scribes, artisans,
down the classes
to the bottom rungs
where toiled the farmers,
servants, and slaves.

Impossible gap
from pharaoh to the bottom,
but common folk knew how
to stretch their pay.
Those few sacks of grain a month,
perhaps a bit of copper,
might be enough, might be enough
to barter for clothes
or save up
for some chickens.

People liked their daily bread
laced with onions, garlic, figs,
meat when they could get it.
Sometimes a dance,
a song or two,
a game to make things brighter.

Life was hard, often brief,
in ancient Egypt,
especially for common folk
on the bottom rungs.

Cradle of Civilization—Mesopotamia
(3100–539 B.C.E.)

By David L. Harrison

Mesopotamia,
how shall we know you,
ancient "land between rivers?"

Between Euphrates
and mighty Tigris—
mountains, deserts, marshes,

Home to fishermen,
herders of goats,
tribesmen, nomads, villagers.

Mesopotamia,
we shall call you,
"Cradle of Civilization."

Home to scholars,
mathematicians,
students of stars and writing.

Some distant day
your history will feed
many differing cultures—

Iraq, Iran,
Syria, Turkey—
the heritage of Mesopotamia.

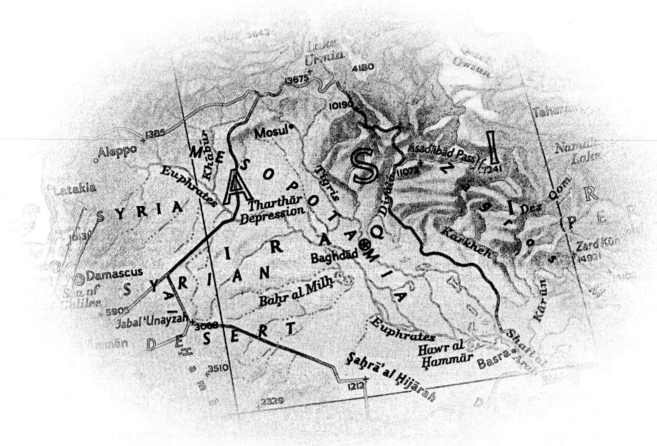

Sacred Cows—India
(apx. 3000 B.C.E.)

By David L. Harrison

There's something about a cow . . .
her patience perhaps,
the calm way she sways about
her business—
chewing, chewing,
tail switching absent mindedly,
as though digesting important thoughts
with her food.

Long ago,
in a place called Indus Valley,
a man who owned a cow
was a man of means.
His generous cow gave him milk,
dung for his fire,
fertilized his field,
pulled his plow.

As thousands of years passed,
Hindus came to believe
that cattle were more than mere beasts—
they were symbols of strength,
selfless giving, abundance.
Cattle, they said, were sacred.

Since those early times
sacred cows of India
roam where they please,
munching handouts,
chewing, chewing,
tails switching absent mindedly,
as though digesting their food
with important thoughts.

Gifts of the Mayans (2600 B.C.E.)

By David L. Harrison

Early Mayans figured out
the absence of something—
　　(the lack of something)
　　(the missing of something)—
meant something.

It meant "nothing."
They gave "nothing"
its own symbol
so "nothing" equals zero.

They took the calendar,
an old idea,
and made it better
so they could measure
passing time,
past, present,
and remote future.

Hundreds of thousands
of Mayans lived
across Belize,
the Yucatan Peninsula,
and left us valuable gifts.

They left us "nothing"
and a better way
of marking time.

Rise and Fall—Babylon
(2300–539 B.C.E.)

By David L. Harrison

From a small village 4,000 years ago
you grew to a mighty city state,
a warrior state,
powerful, bold, proud,
the "holy city" of Mesopotamia.

Once you were called Babylonia,
"gateway of the gods,"
one of history's greatest centers of learning,
home to kings like Nebuchadnezzar,
extravagant, wealthy people.

Famous for your beauty,
canals, temples, lavish palaces,
the mighty Euphrates River

flowing through your midst—

Today you lie in ruins,
deserted streets,
crumbling murals,
lonely debris.

Babylon.
The grandeur that once was
lives now only
in history.

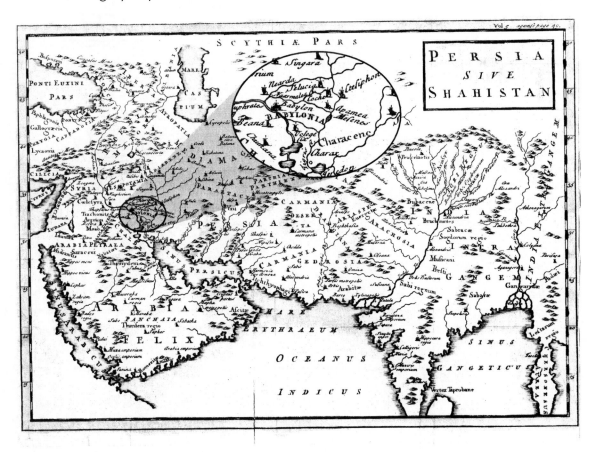

If This Temple Could Talk—Mayans
(2000 B.C.E.)

By David L. Harrison

Thousands of years ago
temple priests plied their trade
from this height of supreme power.
They studied the heavens,
worshipped chosen gods.
When it fit their purpose,
they plucked out beating
human hearts.

Perched atop this pyramid's
brawny shoulders,
its old secrets cloaked
by vine-hung trees,
the temple now hosts
howler monkeys,
toucans, bees.

Biblical—Israelites (1500 B.C.E.)

By David L. Harrison

In the Land of Canaan
lived Jacob,
grandson of Abraham,
whose sons founded tribes,
became a kingdom,
worshiped God,
built temples,
created sacred records.

They lived in times of violent battles,
cities at war,
kingdoms toppling kingdoms.
Stories tell of great temptations,
courage, patience, rewards.

Though tongues of the ancients
speak no more
their voices yet are heard,
revealing themselves in stories,
tales, parables from the past.

Archaeology—Israelites (1500 B.C.E.)

By David L. Harrison

Thirty-five hundred years ago
there lived in the near east
a tribe known as Israelites.

Much is written about these people,
how they multiplied, formed villages,
fell to the Egyptians,
became enslaved, escaped,
followed Moses into the wilderness,
built Solomon's Temple.

Archaeologists seek proof,
traces of the old stories,
clues in the wilderness,
evidence to help decide
between fact and fiction.

So much is still to know
about those distant tribesmen
whose beliefs and traditions
influence today the lives
of so many millions.

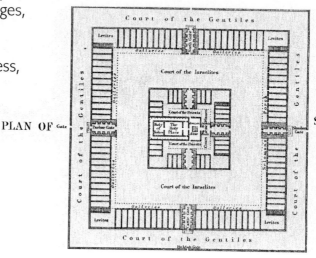

PLAN OF SOLOMON'S TEMPLE

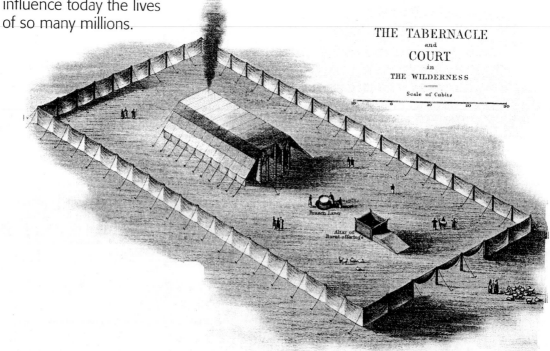

THE TABERNACLE
and
COURT
in
THE WILDERNESS

Scale of Cubits

Oracle Bones from the Shang Dynasty— Ancient China (1200 B.C.E.)

By David L. Harrison

In olden Anyang this is what they said.
The future could be told by reading bones.
But only wise men knew how they were read.

Priests would ask the bones what lay ahead
By scratching questions known to them alone.
In olden Anyang this is what they said.

They heated sticks so they were burning red
And stuck them into holes laid out in zones.
But only wise men knew how they were read.

Sometimes they asked their questions of the dead,
Questions ancient spirits should have known.
In olden Anyang this is what they said.

When kings demanded what might lie ahead,
Good answers made them easy on their thrones.
But only wise men knew how they were read.

Better to know than leave the truth unsaid.
Cracks from the heat were how the truth was shown.
In olden Anyang this is what they said.
But only wise men knew how they were read.

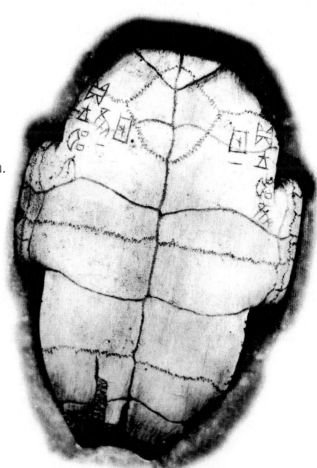

The Olympics Begin—Greece (776 B.C.E.)

By David L. Harrison

On the ancient plains of Olympia,
strong athletes ran, wrestled,
hurled stones, fought, boxed,
tested their strength, nerve, endurance,
respected the Olympian gods,
represented their cities in peace.

Champions earned red ribbons,
palm branches to carry,
sacred olive wreaths upon their heads,
the cheers of adoring fans.

Single women could come to watch.
The priestess of Demeter—
goddess of fertility—
sat in a place of honor.
But married women?
Strictly forbidden
to attend such masculine displays.

Athens—Greece (479-323 B.C.E.)

By David L. Harrison

And during that golden age
they built the Parthenon,
and Athens,
mighty Athens,
was in its glory.

They built it all of marble
for their patron goddess Athena,
goddess of wisdom, justice, war,
who was born, they said,
full grown out of Zeus's head.

And during that golden age,
Socrates taught Plato
and Plato taught Aristotle.

And Athens,
mighty Athens,
produced art and literature,
philosophy, democracy,
influenced all the Western World
like few before.

School—Rome
(300 B.C.E.)

By David L. Harrison

Imagine being a kid in Rome
Where education starts at home,
Learning basics you will need—
To do math, write, read . . .

School is nothing like today,
You have no tests along the way.
Your school is anywhere you meet,
A house, a public place, a street.

Students practice on their own.
Often you are left alone
To read Latin, practice Greek.
You study seven days a week!

To prove your mastery you must show
Your teacher everything you know.
There's much to learn in ancient Rome,
And education starts at home.

Terra-cotta Army—China (250 B.C.E.)

By David L. Harrison

The silent ancient army marches on
Yet neither lifts a boot nor raises dust,
Armed to fight in ages long gone,
Still ready to do its duty if it must.

Eight thousand strong plus chariots and horses,
They guard the tomb where lies the emperor Qin,
Wondrous warriors, terra-cotta forces,
Forever there, his ever-faithful men.

Julius Caesar—Rome (46–44 B.C.E.)

By David L. Harrison

Caesar himself,
so it was said,
hated the ruckus—
    chariots rattling stony streets,
    dogs yapping, screaming boys,
    vendors shouting, crowded shops,
    roaring hubbub, thrumming noise—
"Enough!"

Caesar might have said—
    pounding hoof beats, beggars' cries,
    bleating animals, shrieks, squeals,
    cracking whips, roaring crowds,
    warlike groaning iron wheels—

"I cannot think!"
    All was jangle, throb, and clamor,
    Clatter, chatter, clang, and clop.
    Caesar must have held his head
    and longed to make the noises stop.

The biggest city on the earth,
a million people called it home.
"It's noisy here," said Caesar.
It was Rome!

The Colosseum—Rome (80 C.E.)

By David L. Harrison

Exploding roars! Jeers!
Hoots heard for miles!
Fifty thousand lusty throats
cheer the greatest show on Earth
in the Colosseum!

Gladiators circle warily,
trained warriors ready to fight,
armed to maim,
ready to die to amuse the crowd.

At other times there will be a play,
wild beasts in the ring,
mock sea battles,
executions.

But not today—
Today it's gladiators!

Exploding roars! Jeers!
Hoots heard for miles!
Fifty thousand lusty throats
cheer the greatest show on Earth
in the Colosseum!

Appendices

Correlation to the Standards

Shell Education is committed to producing educational materials that are research and standards based. In this effort, we have correlated all of our products to the academic standards of all 50 states, the District of Columbia, the Department of Defense Dependents Schools, and all Canadian provinces.

How to Find Standards Correlations

To print a customized correlation report of this product for your state, visit our website at http://www.shelleducation.com and follow the on-screen directions. If you require assistance in printing correlation reports, please contact our Customer Service Department at 1-877-777-3450.

Purpose and Intent of Standards

Legislation mandates that all states adopt academic standards that identify the skills students will learn in kindergarten through grade twelve. Many states also have standards for Pre–K. This same legislation sets requirements to ensure the standards are detailed and comprehensive.

Standards are designed to focus instruction and guide adoption of curricula. Standards are statements that describe the criteria necessary for students to meet specific academic goals. They define the knowledge, skills, and content students should acquire at each level. Standards are also used to develop standardized tests to evaluate students' academic progress. Teachers are required to demonstrate how their lessons meet state standards. State standards are used in the development of all of our products, so educators can be assured they meet the academic requirements of each state.

TESOL and WIDA Standards

The activities in this book promote English language development for English language learners. The following TESOL and WIDA standards are addressed through the activities in this book:

- **Standard 1:** English language learners **communicate** for **social**, **intercultural**, and **instructional** purposes within the school setting.

- **Standard 2:** English language learners **communicate** information, ideas, and concepts necessary for academic success in the area of **language arts**.

- **Standard 5:** English language learners **communicate** information, ideas and concepts necessary for academic success in the content area of **Social Studies**.

Correlation to the Standards *(cont.)*

College and Career Readiness Anchor Standards	Strategies
Read closely to determine what the text says explicitly and to make logical inferences from it; cite specific textual evidence when writing or speaking to support conclusions drawn from the text. (R.1)	• Teacher-Provided Reader's Theater (p. 14) • Word Ladders (p. 26) • Closed Word Sorts (p. 31) • Greek and Latin Roots (p. 46) • WORD-O (p. 52) • Word Whiz (p. 58) • Memory (p. 63) • Connections through Writing (p. 70) • Poetic Form (p. 75)
Determine central ideas or themes of a text and analyze their development; summarize the key supporting details and ideas. (R.2)	• Teacher-Provided Reader's Theater (p. 14) • Student-Written Reader's Theater (p. 20) • Closed Word Sorts (p. 31) • Open Word Sorts (p. 36) • Rhyming Riddles (p. 41) • Word Whiz (p. 58) • Social Studies Content (p. 80)
Interpret words and phrases as they are used in a text, including determining technical, connotative, and figurative meanings, and analyze how specific word choices shape meaning or tone. (R.4)	• Open Word Sorts (p. 36) • WORD-O (p. 52) • Poetic Form (p. 75)
Demonstrate command of the conventions of standard English capitalization, punctuation, and spelling when writing. (L.2)	• Word Ladders (p. 26) • Rhyming Riddles (p. 41)

Correlation to the Standards _(cont.)

College and Career Readiness Anchor Standards	Strategies
Determine or clarify the meaning of unknown and multiple-meaning words and phrases by using context clues, analyzing meaningful word parts, and consulting general and specialized reference materials, as appropriate. (L.4)	• Greek and Latin Roots (p. 46)
Acquire and use accurately a range of general academic and domain-specific words and phrases sufficient for reading, writing, speaking, and listening at the college and career readiness level; demonstrate independence in gathering vocabulary knowledge when encountering an unknown term important to comprehension or expression. (L.6)	• Memory (p. 63) • Social Studies Content (p. 80)
Produce clear and coherent writing in which the development, organization, and style are appropriate to task, purpose, and audience. (W.4)	• Student-Written Reader's Theater (p. 20)
Draw evidence from literary or informational texts to support analysis, reflection, and research. (W.9)	• Connections through Writing (p. 70)

Contents of Digital Resources Online (cont.)

Resource	Filename
Word-O Template	wordo.docx wordo.pdf
Word-O for "New York"	wordo_ny.pdf
Word-O Words and Cards for "New York"	wordo_nycards.pdf
Word Whiz Template	wordwhiz.docx wordwhiz.pdf
Word Whiz for North Carolina	wordwhiz_northcarolina.pdf
Memory Template	memory.docx memory.pdf
Memory for "The Farmer—Neolithic"	memory_farmer.pdf
Connections through Writing Templates	writing.docx writing.pdf
Connections through Writing for "General George Washington"	writing_washington.pdf
Poetic Form Template	poeticform.docx poeticform.pdf
Poetic Form for "Julius Caesar—Rome"	poeticform_caesar.pdf
Guide to Poetic Forms	poeticform_guide.pdf
Social Studies Content Template	socialstudies.docx socialstudies.pdf
Social Studies Content for "Reconstruction"	socialstudies_reconstruction.pdf
Graphic Maps	maps.pdf
Poems and Background Information	poems.pdf
Guidelines for Discussing Poetry	guidelines.pdf